Collected Images

original
photographs

Joseph Fleming

Colorblind Black & White
photography portfolio

Decades of being around accomplished talent producing absolutely phenomenal quality work has taught that we are capable of greatness. It is possible to meet our destiny and become it. Experiencing excellence done with such apparent ease and humble selfless gratification is the motivation for this photography. Most important was having the freedom.

Being colorblind gives an advantage when composing black & white… less confusion. This special collection selected from thousands of captures. All images were framed in the camera and presented without edits, genuine as seen through the lens. Panchromatic conversion applied by unique proprietary process.

Original fine art and custom work available.

info@ BEACHNOISE.com

0125

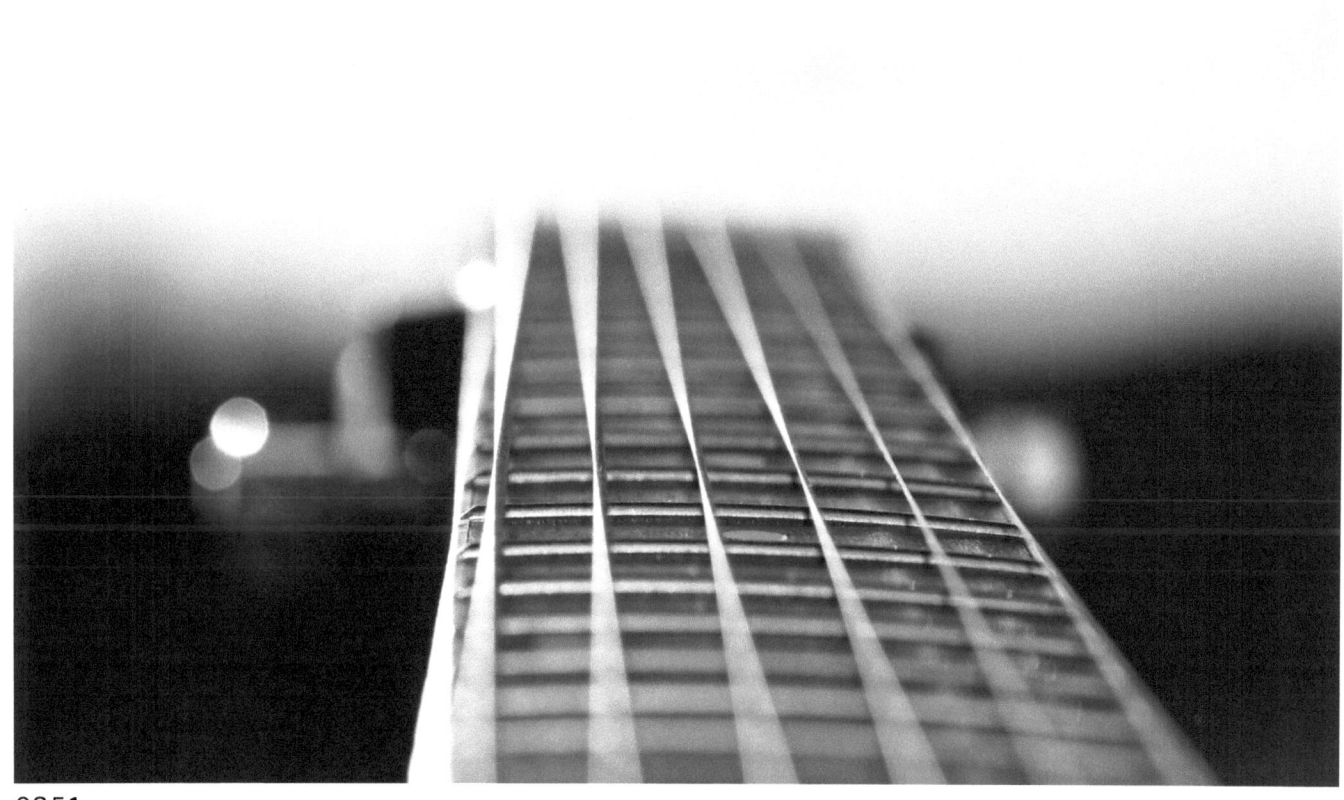

0351

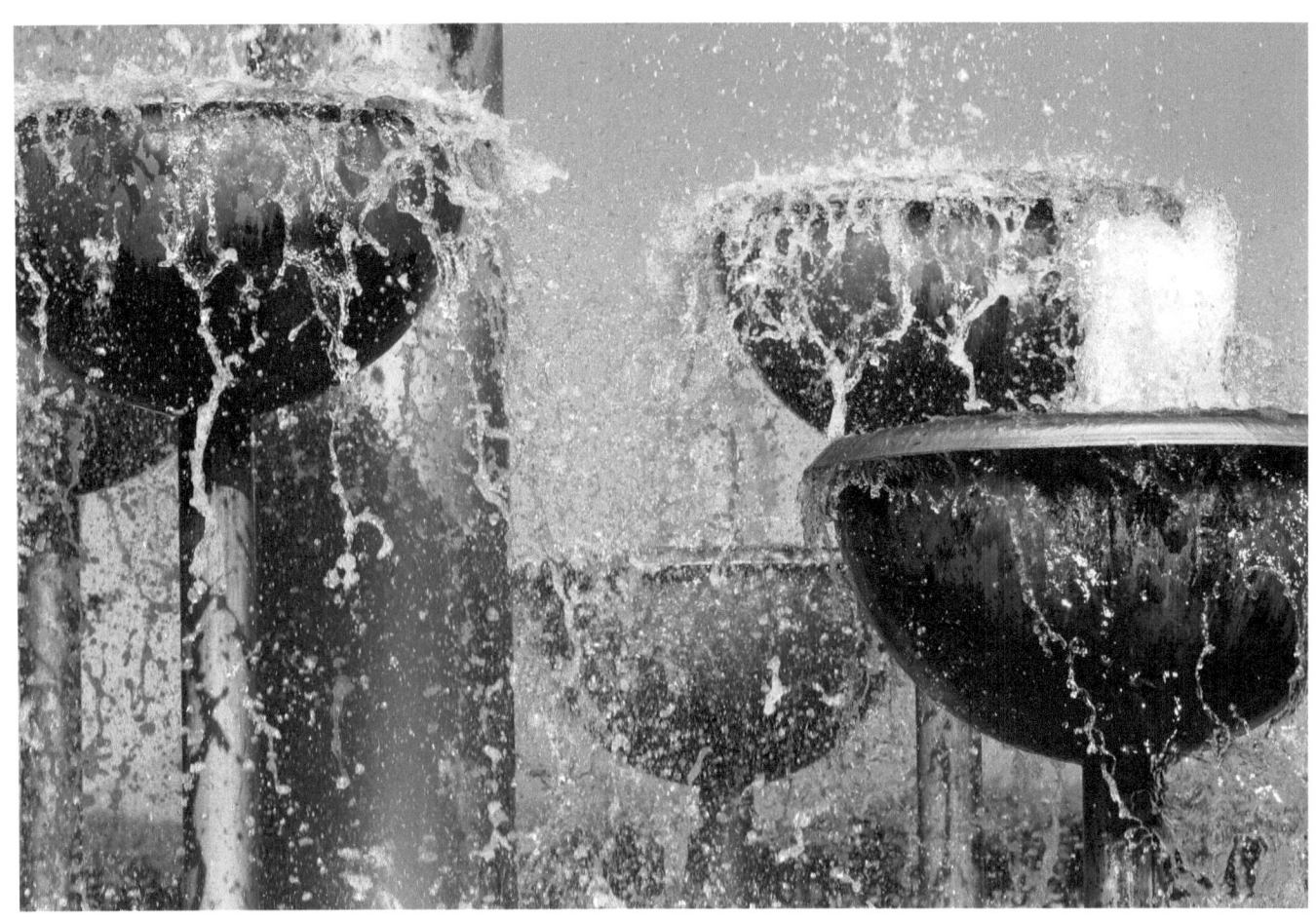

0354

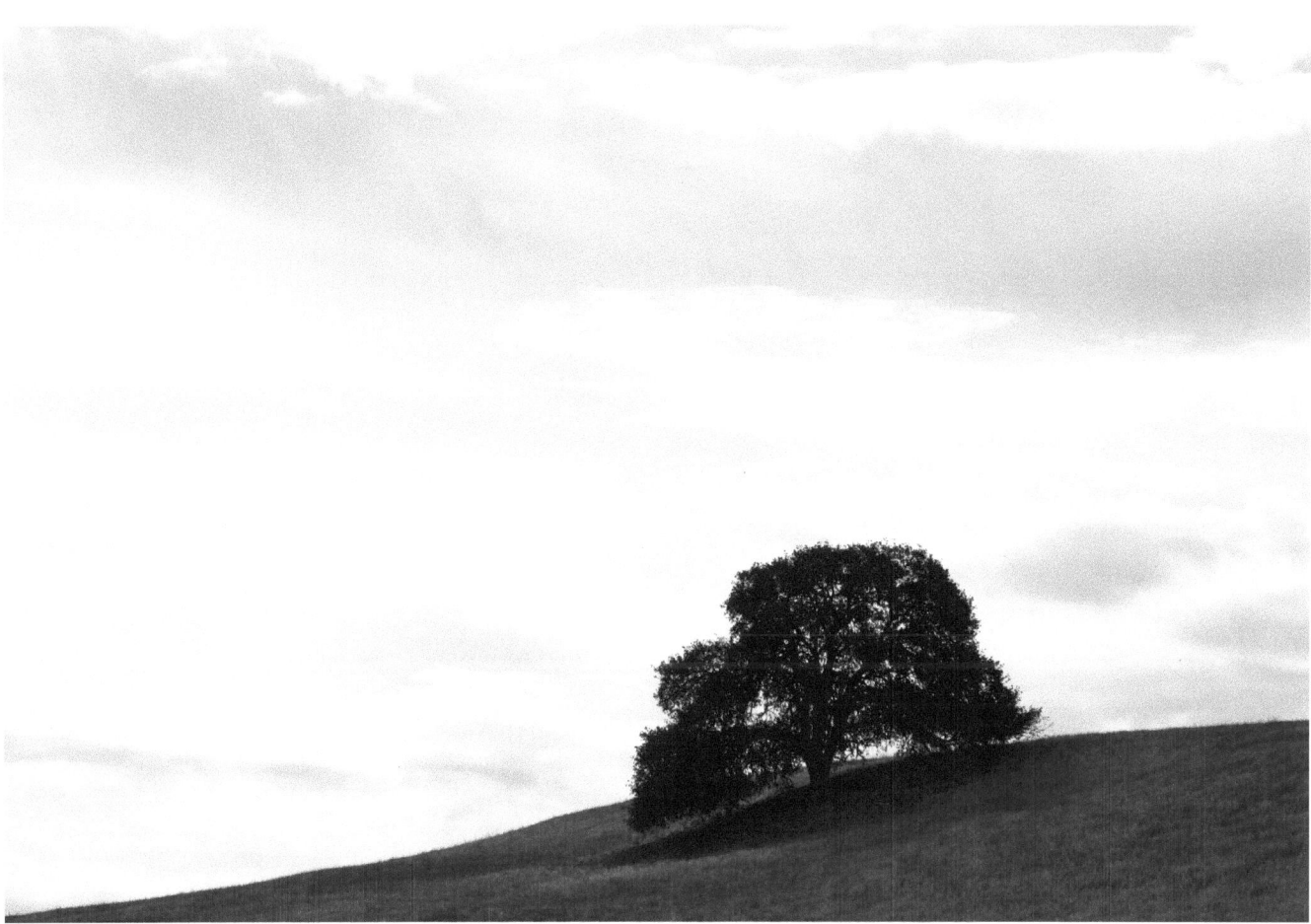

0531

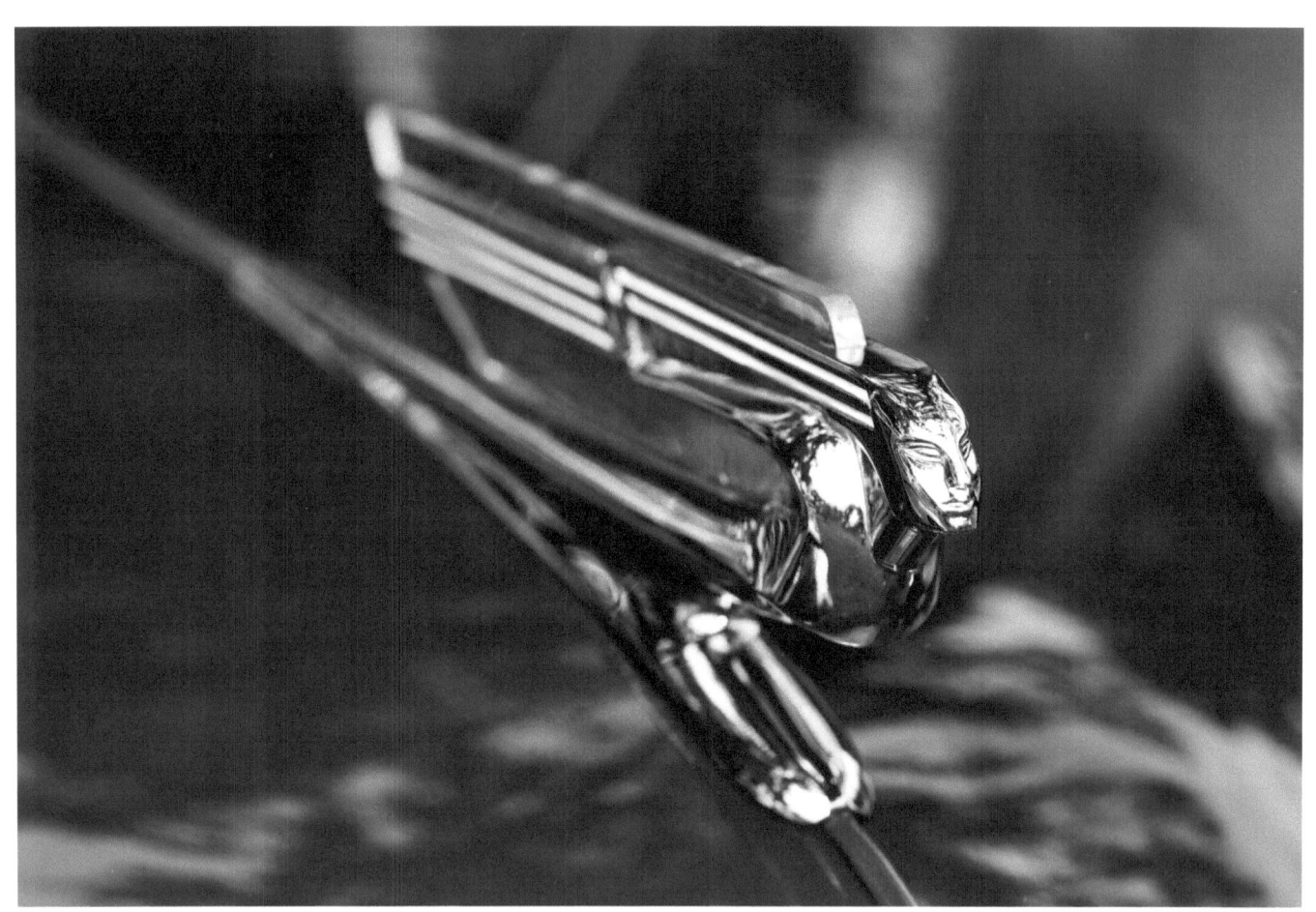

0705

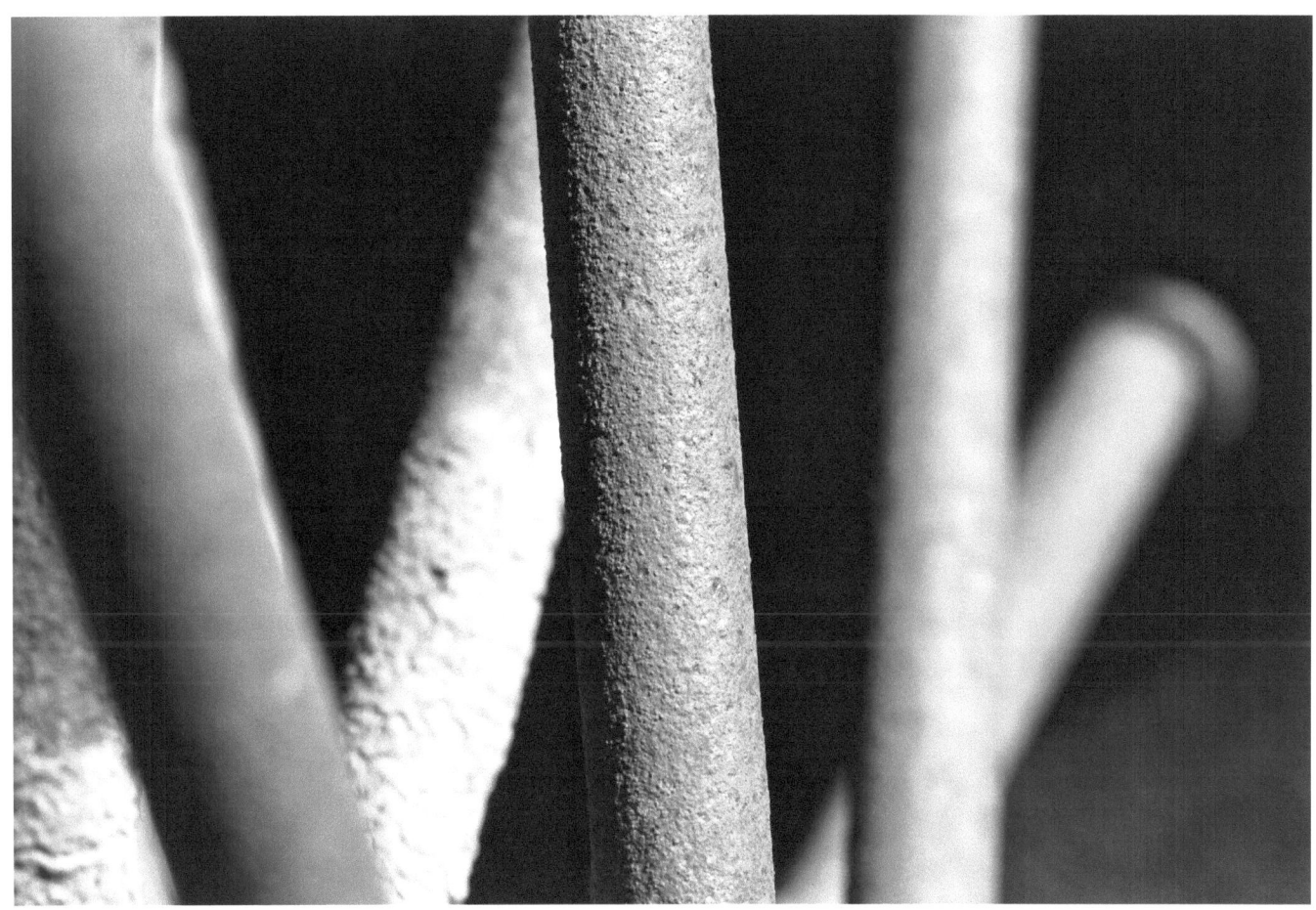

0780

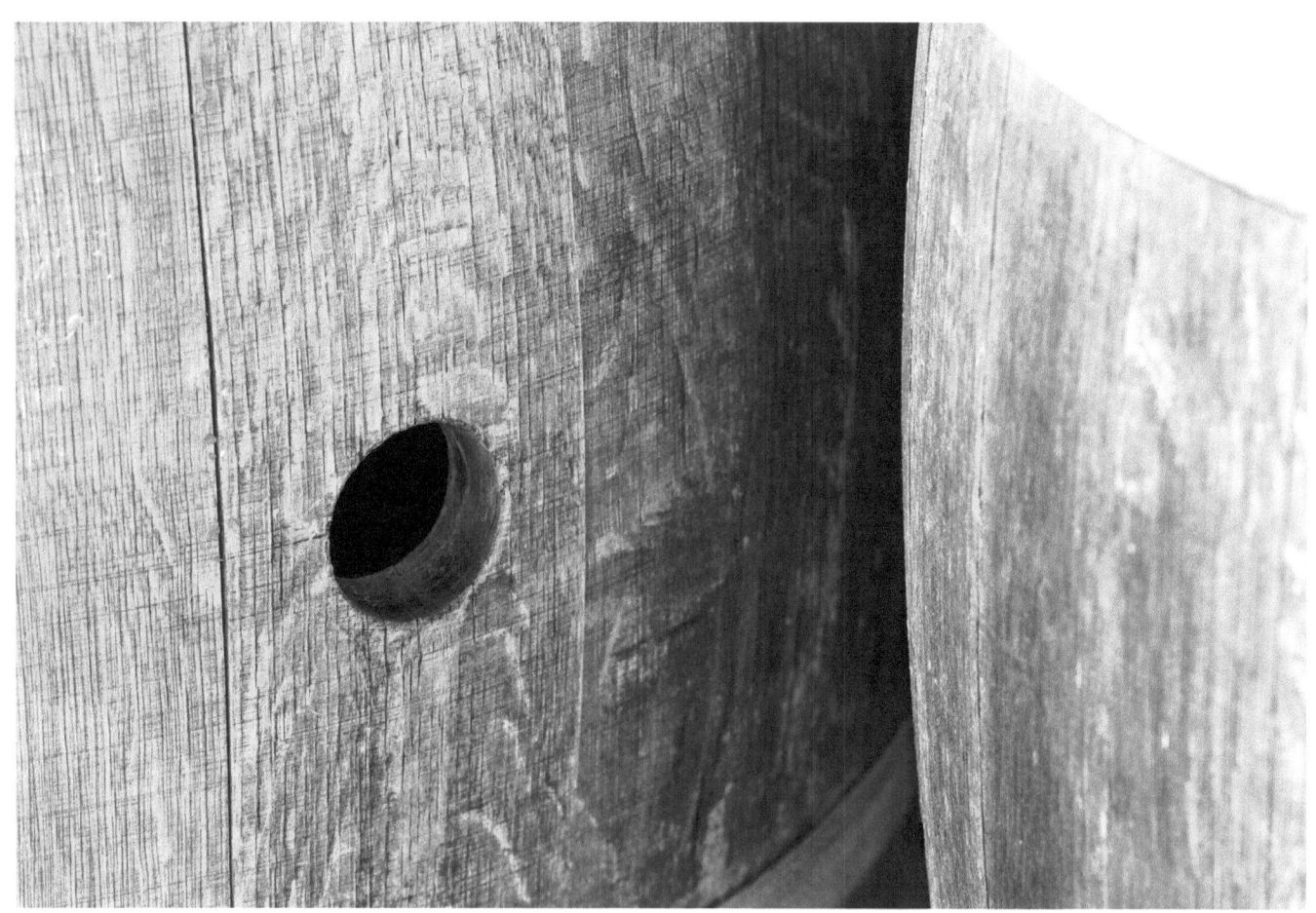

0826

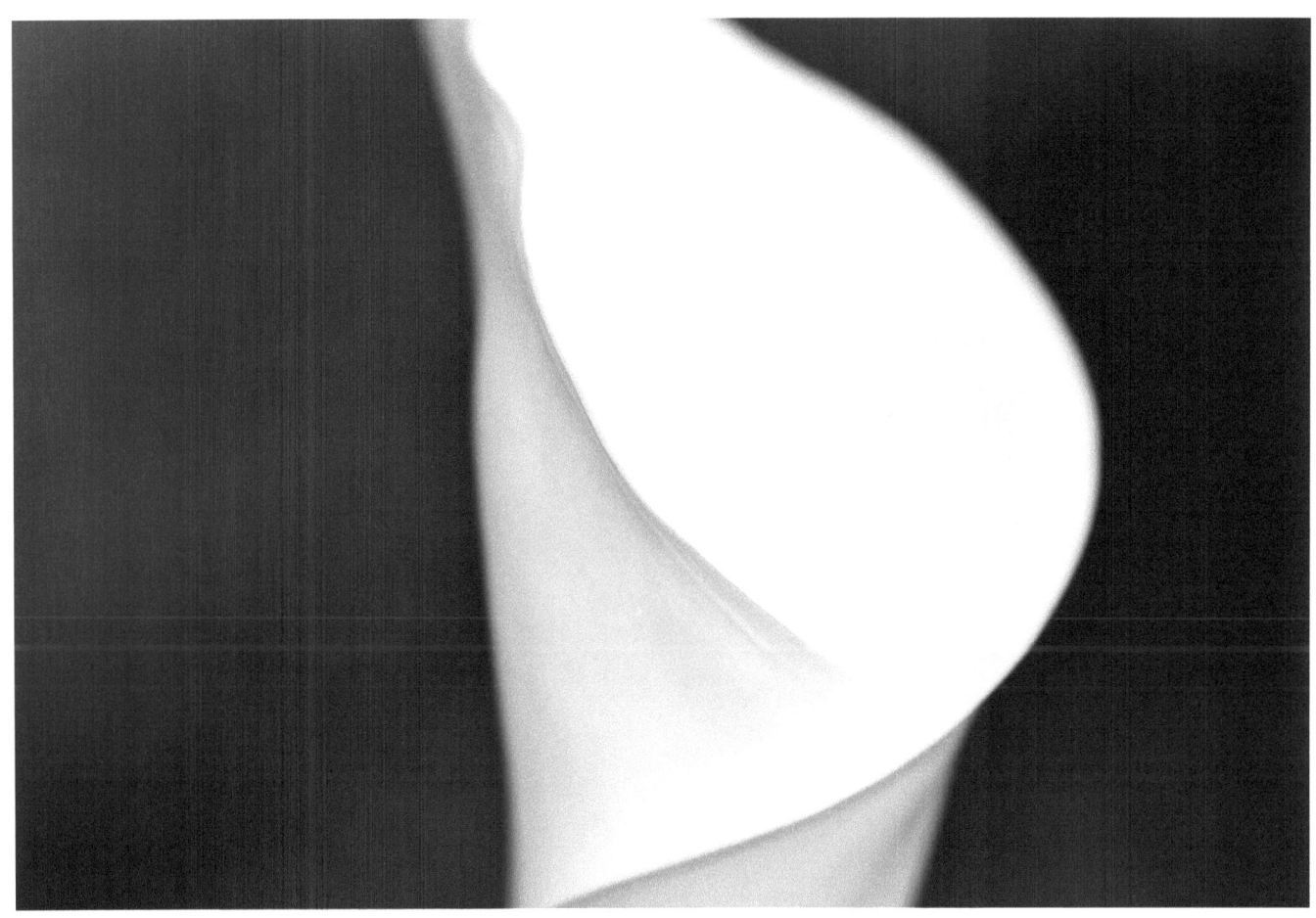

0920

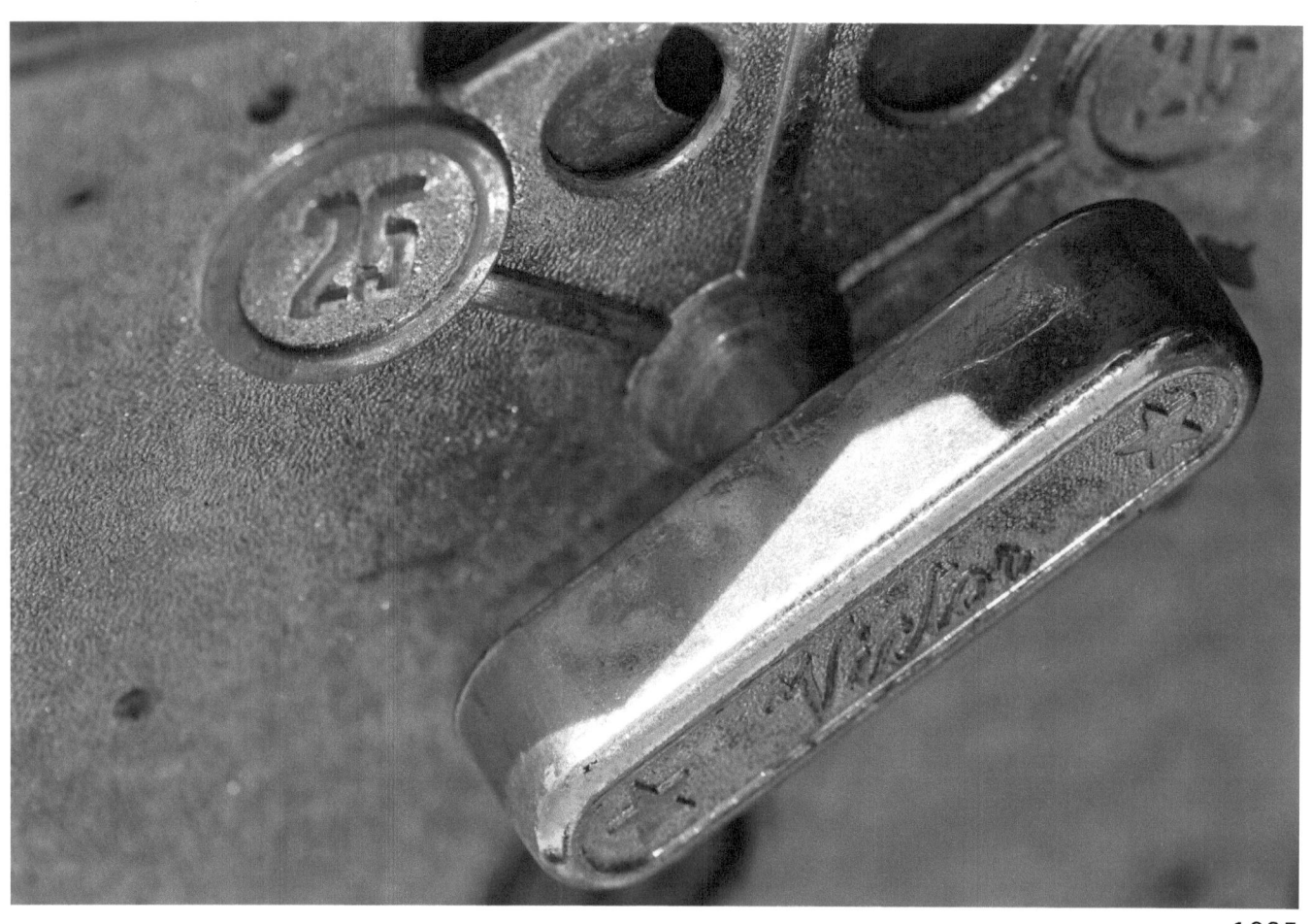

1085

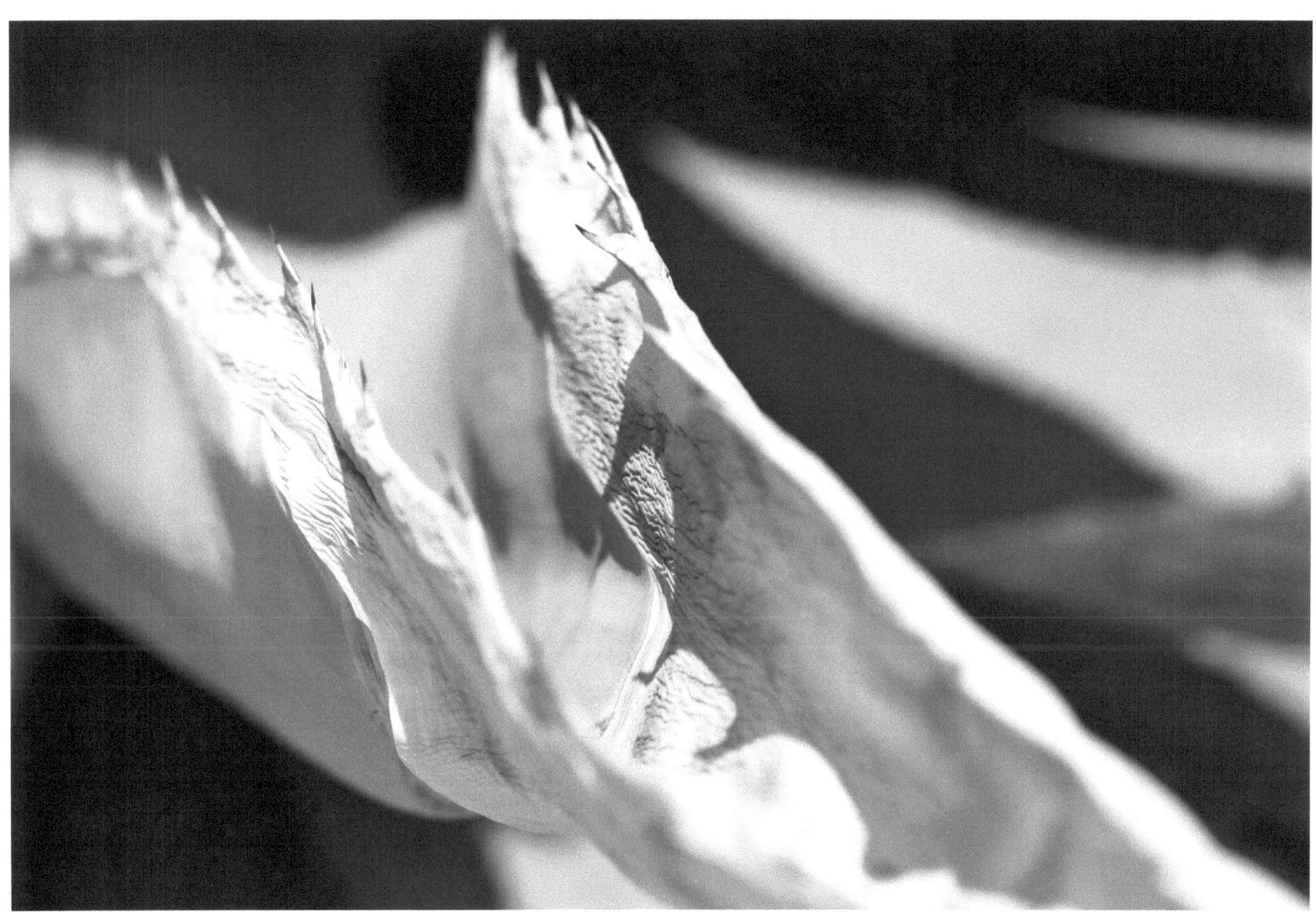

1581

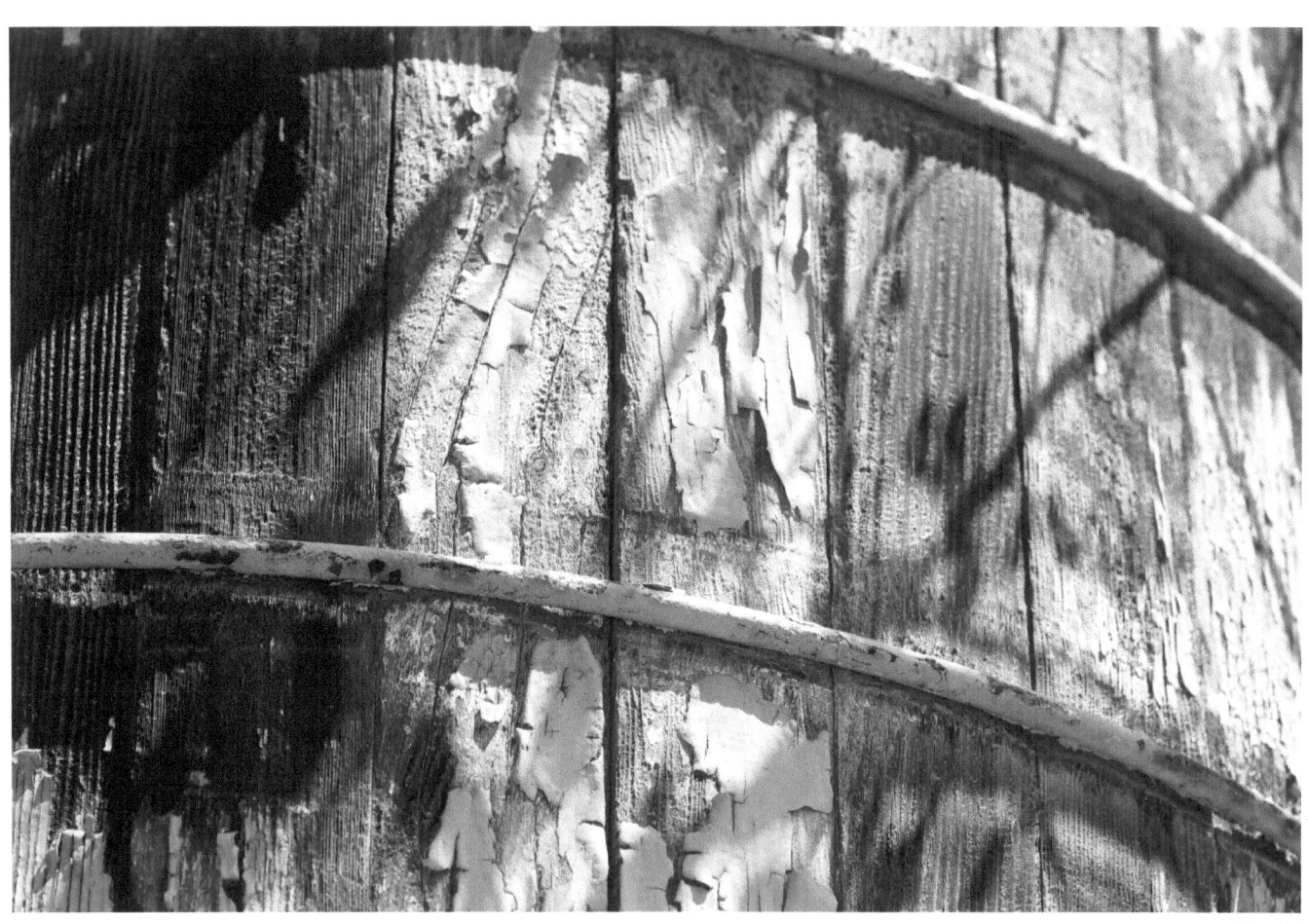

1608

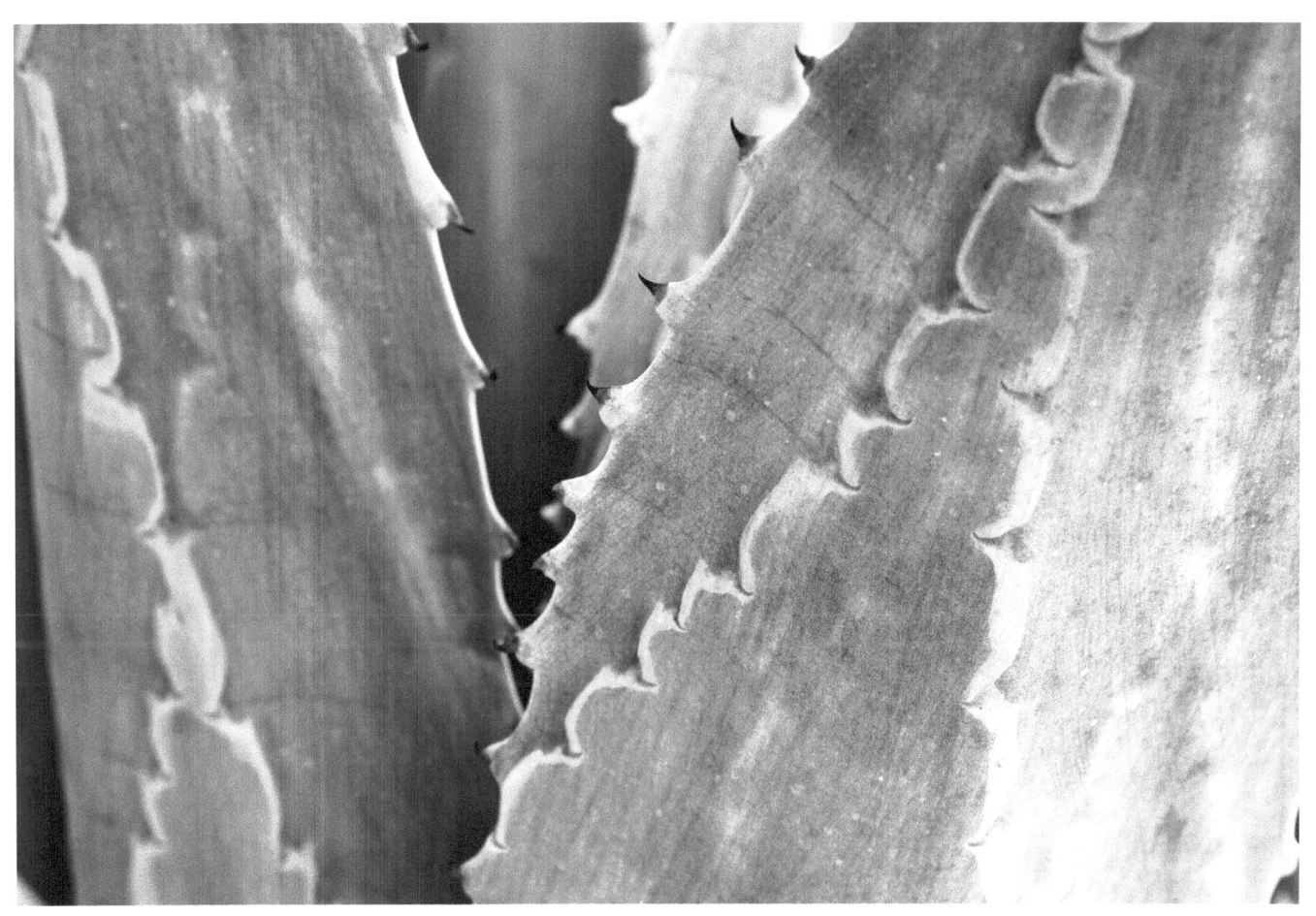

1976

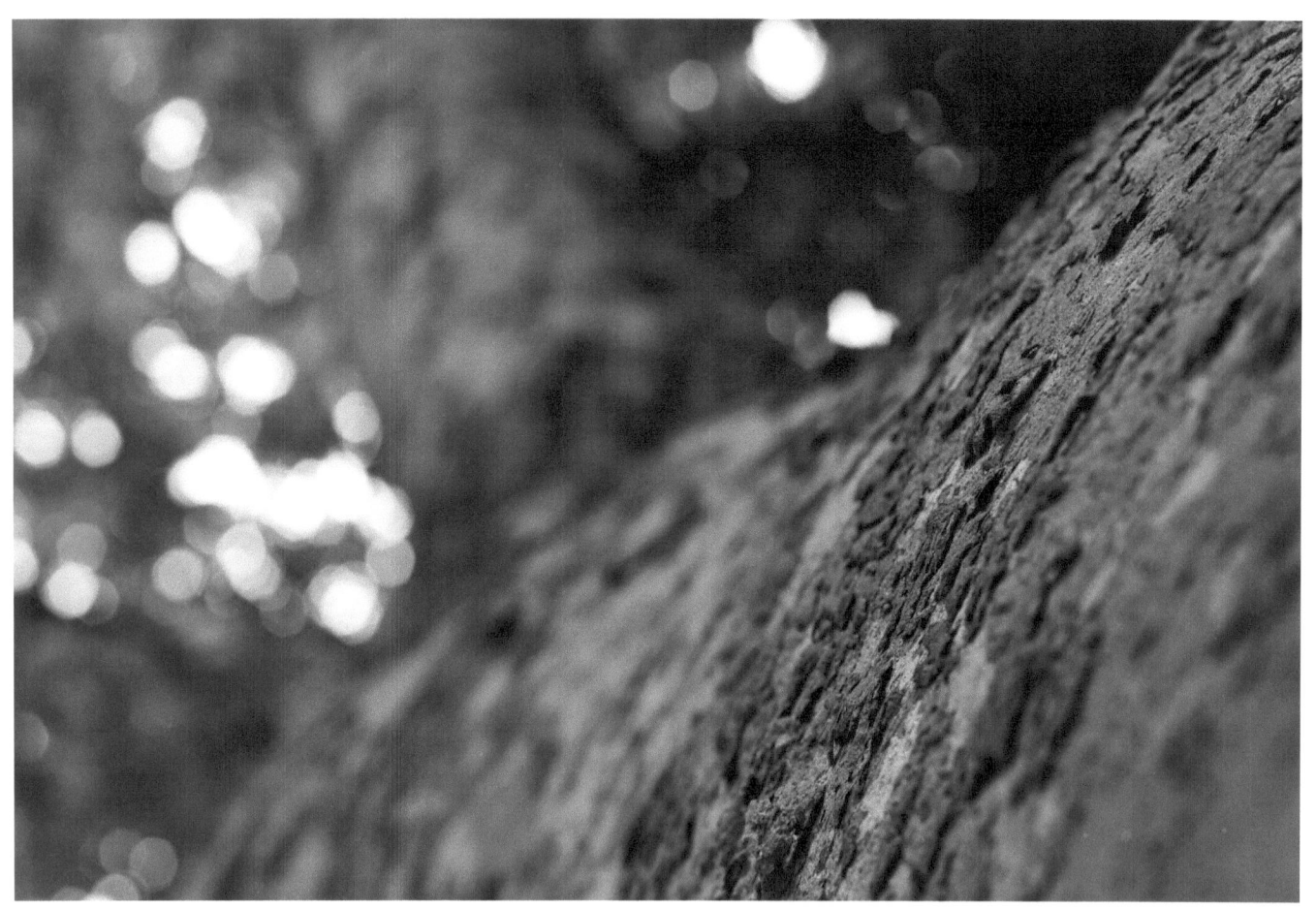

2068

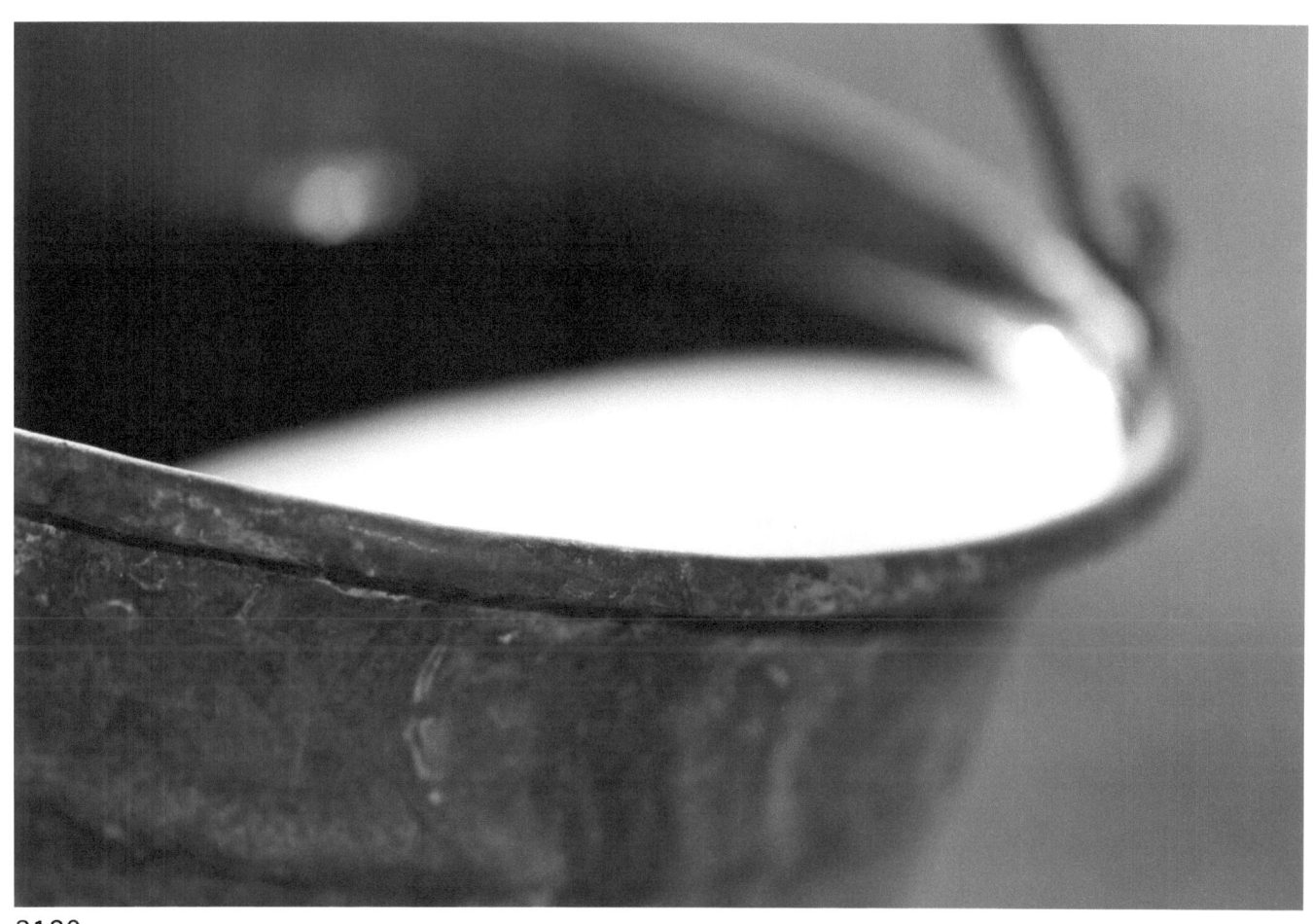

2180

2397

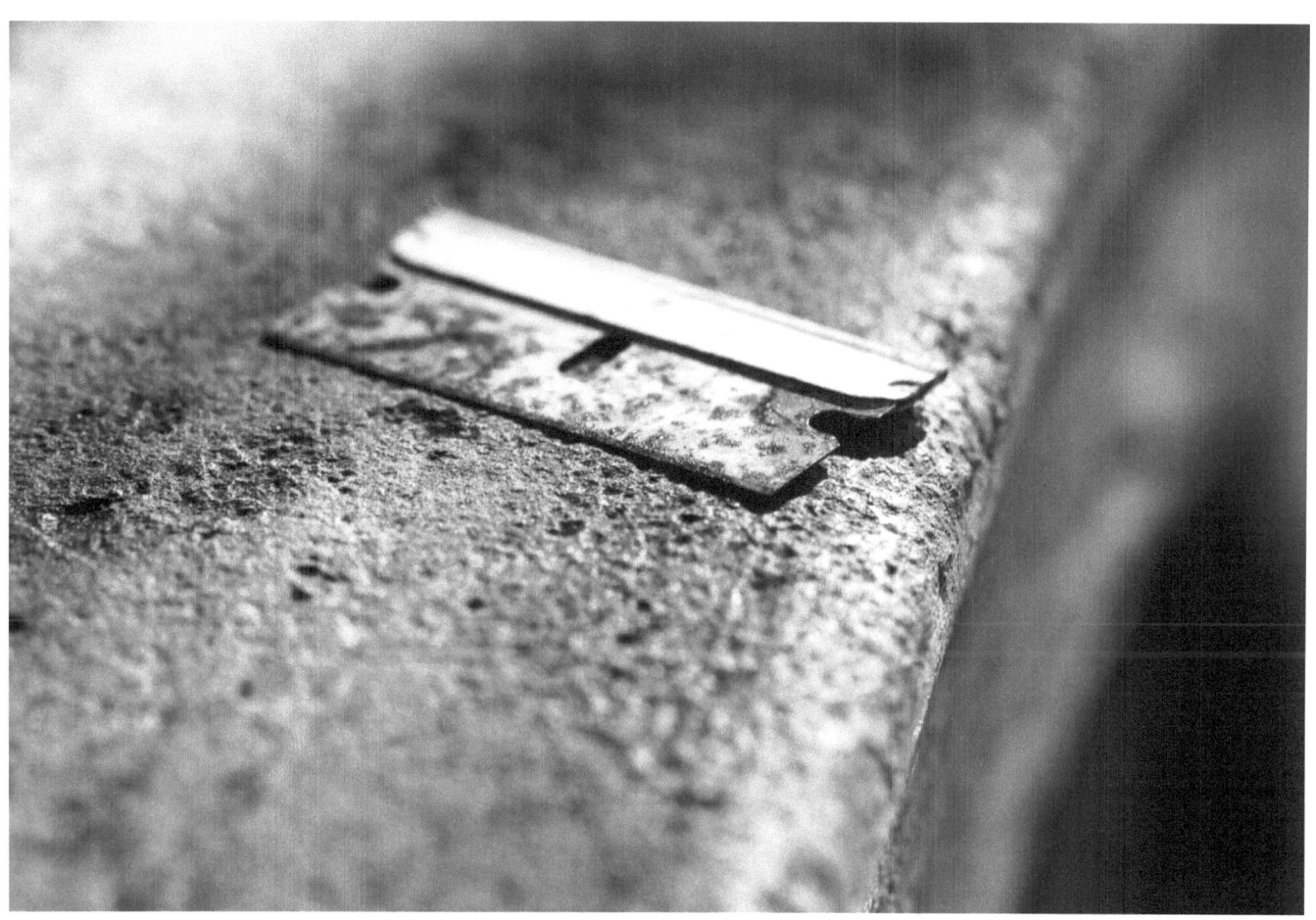

2467

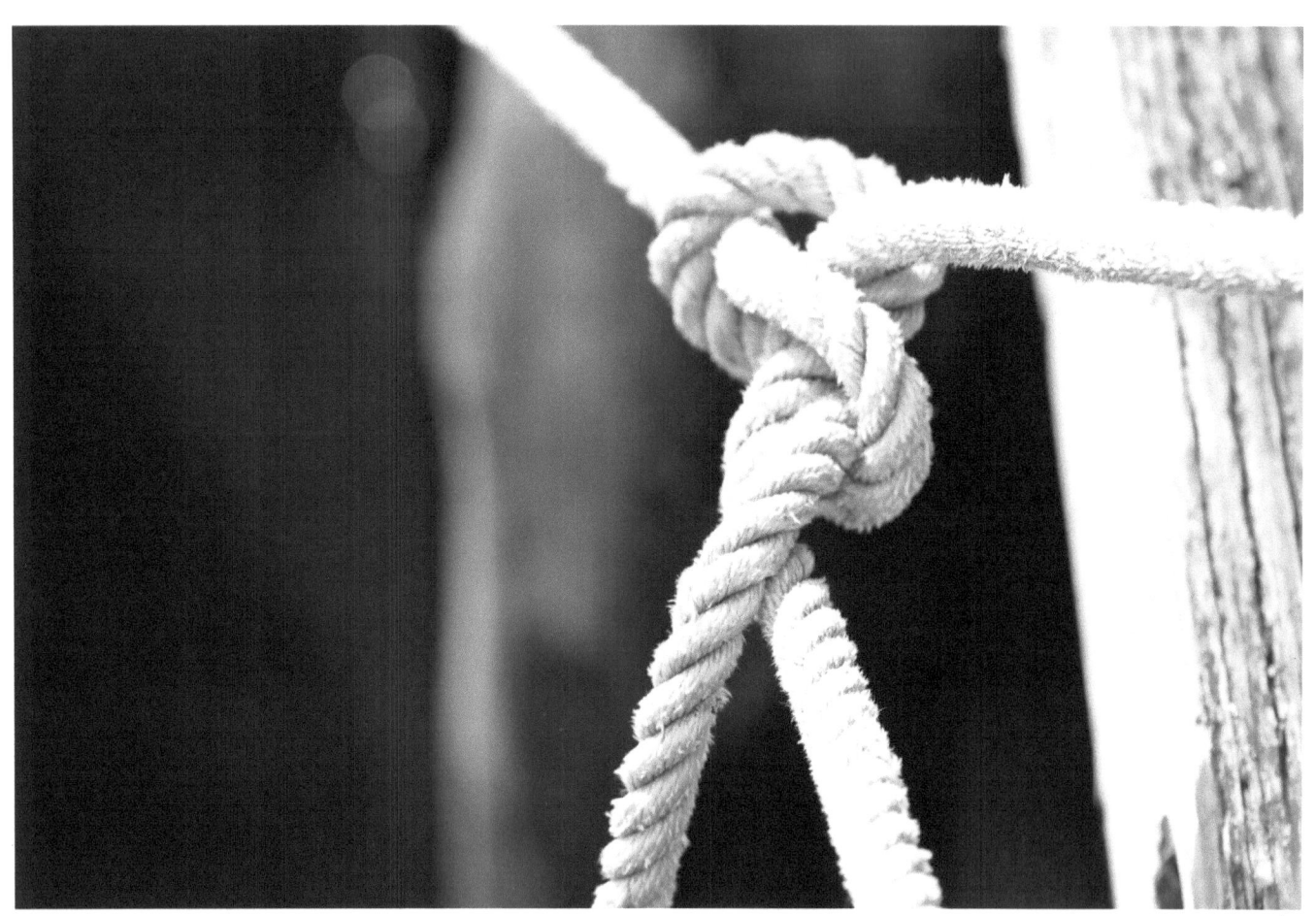

2686

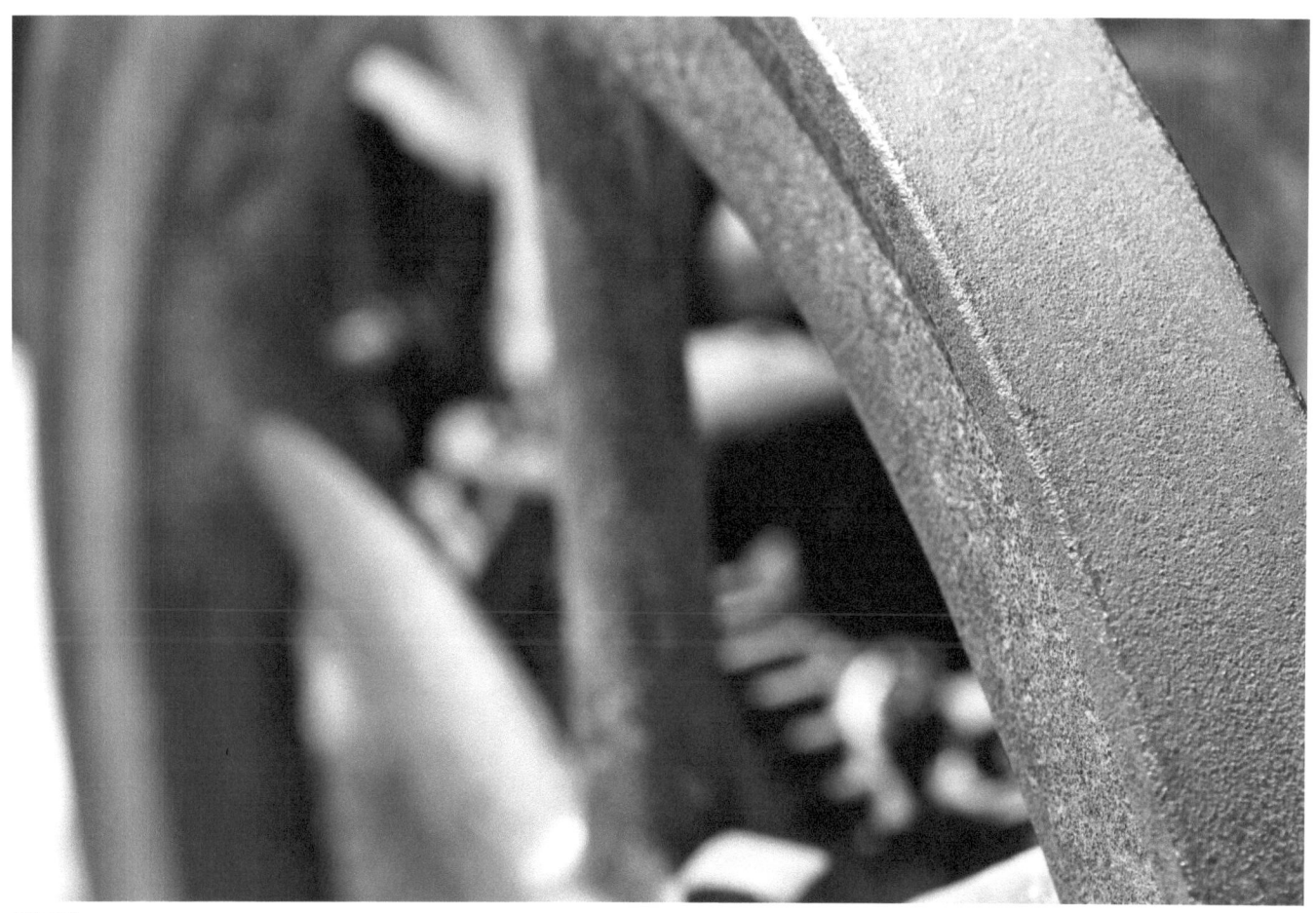

2962

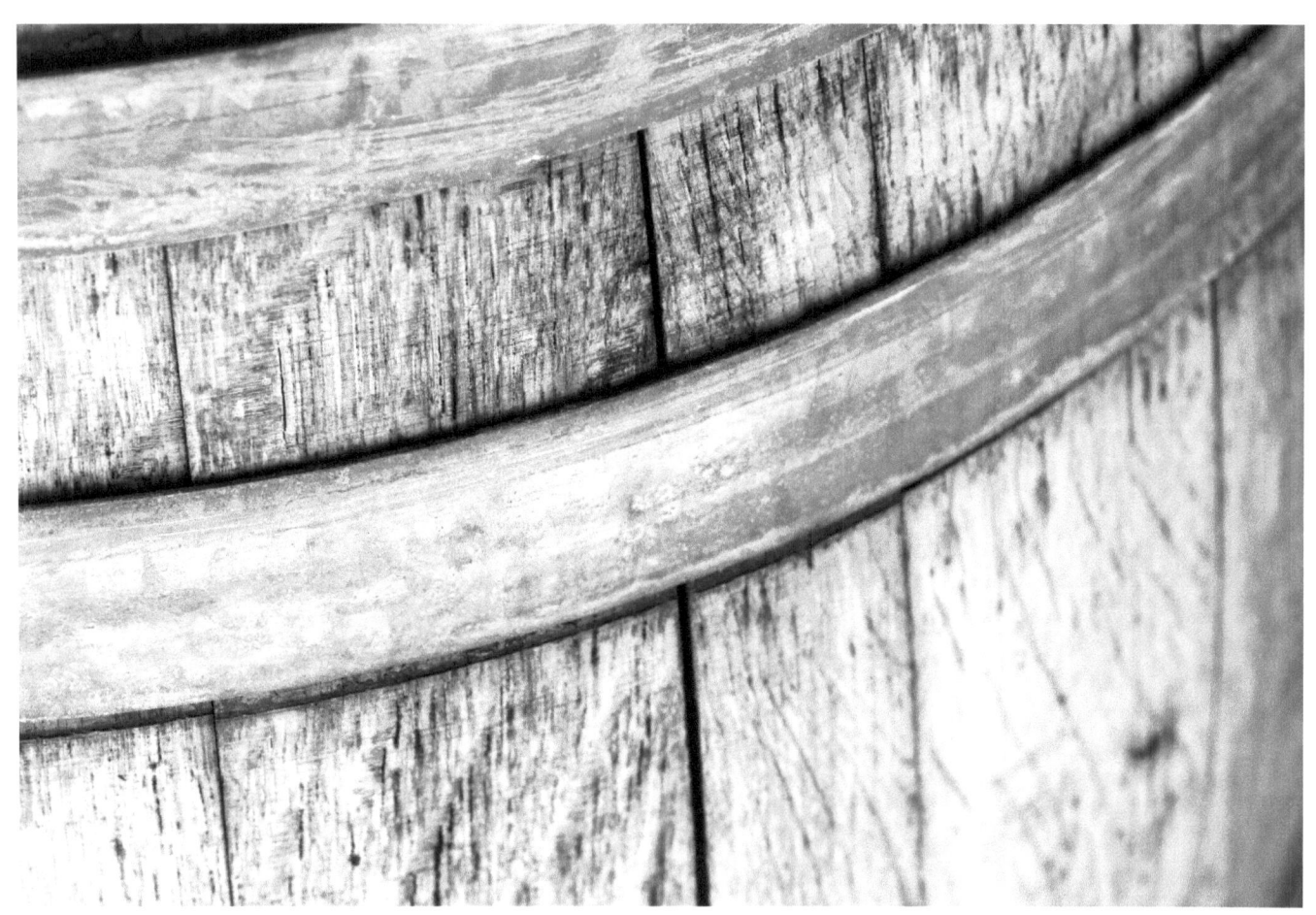

3151

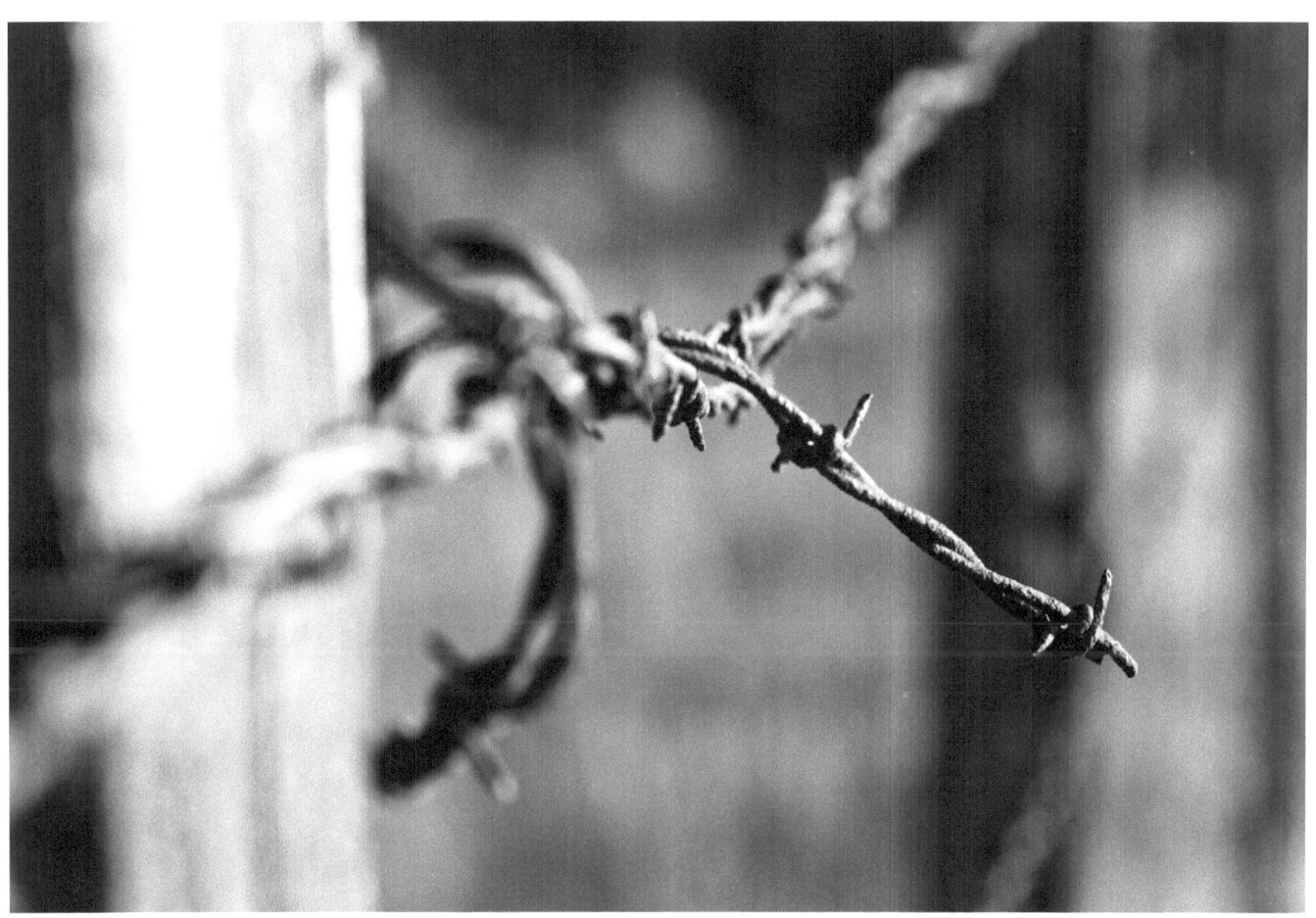

3359

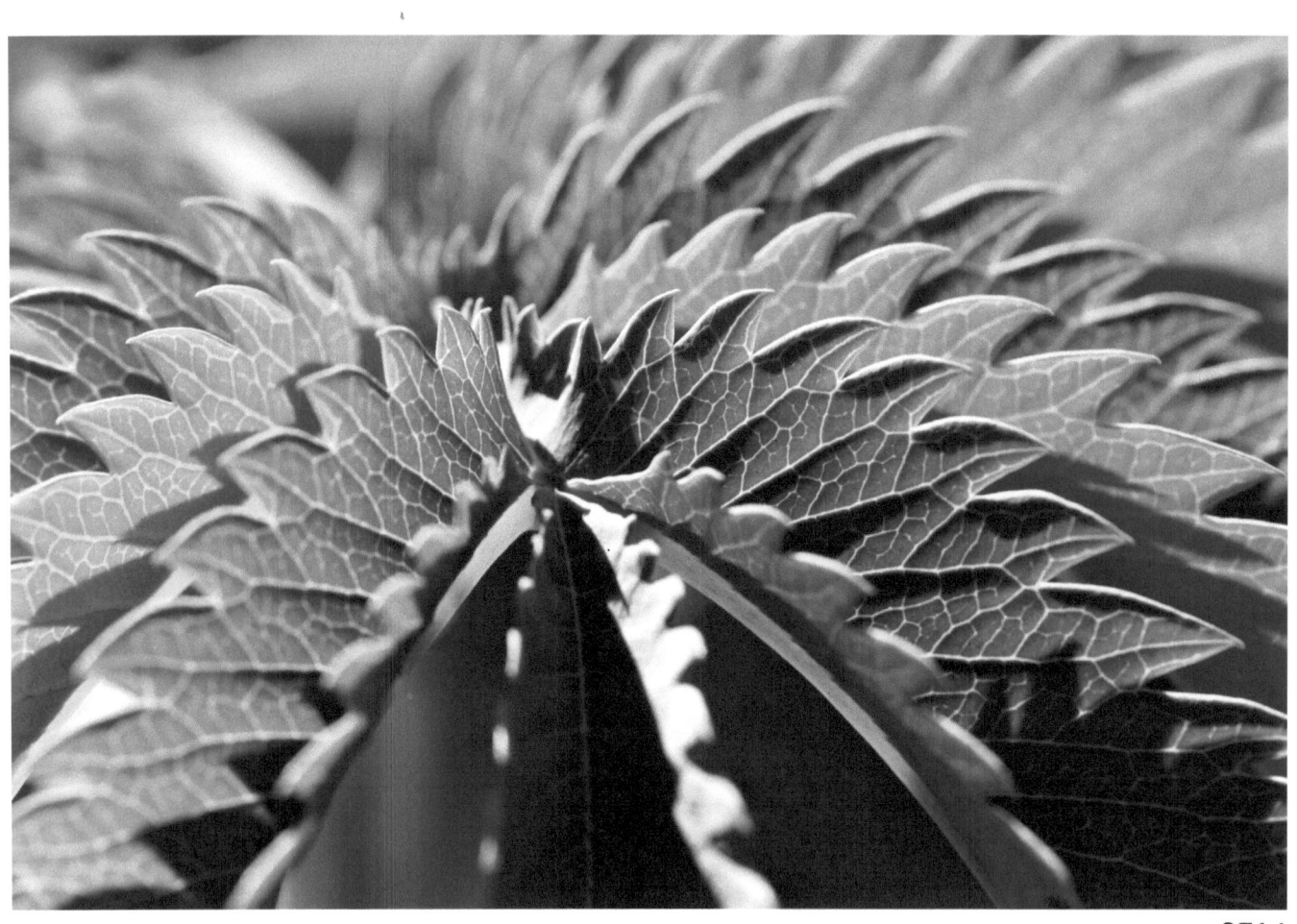

3714

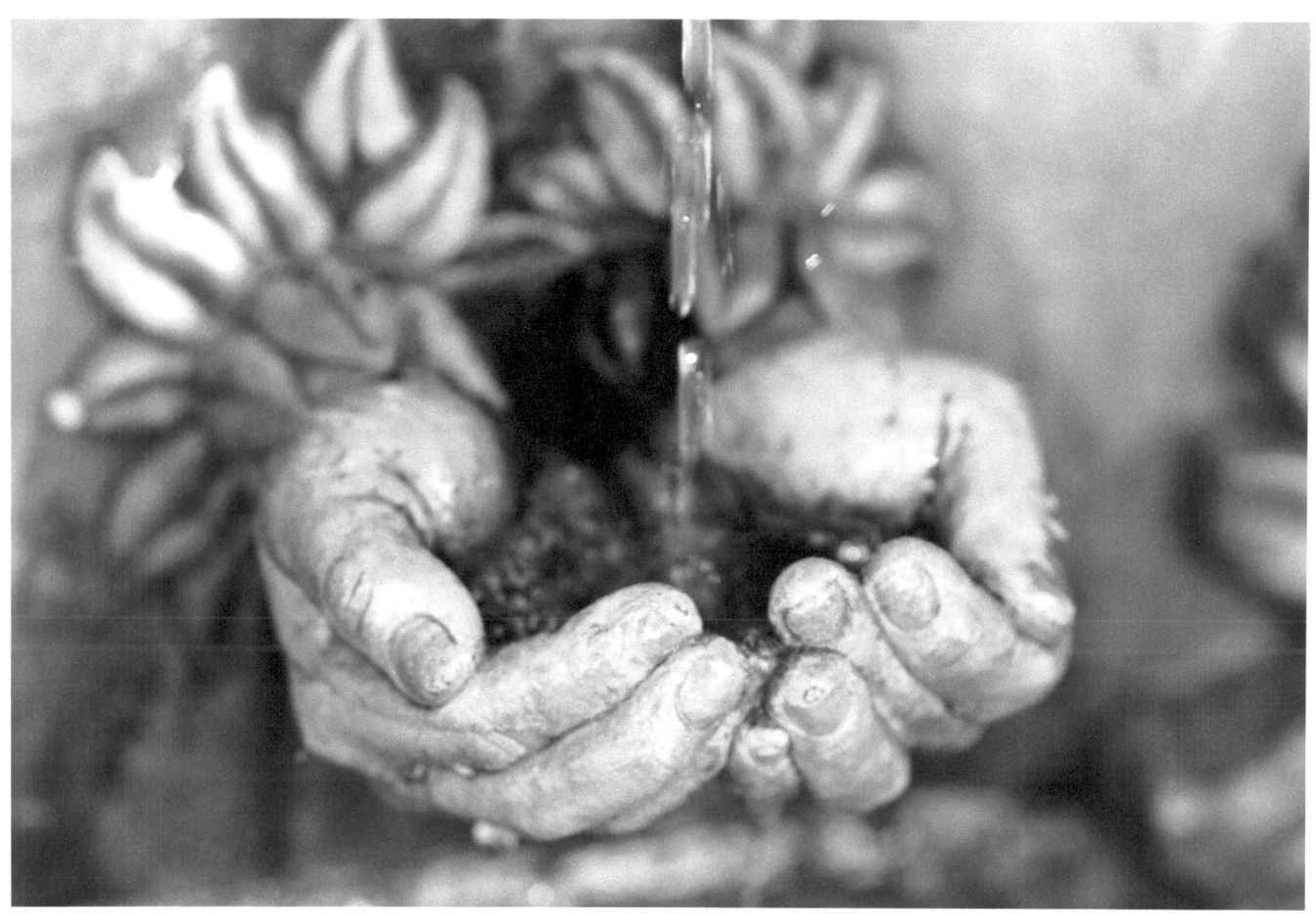

3720

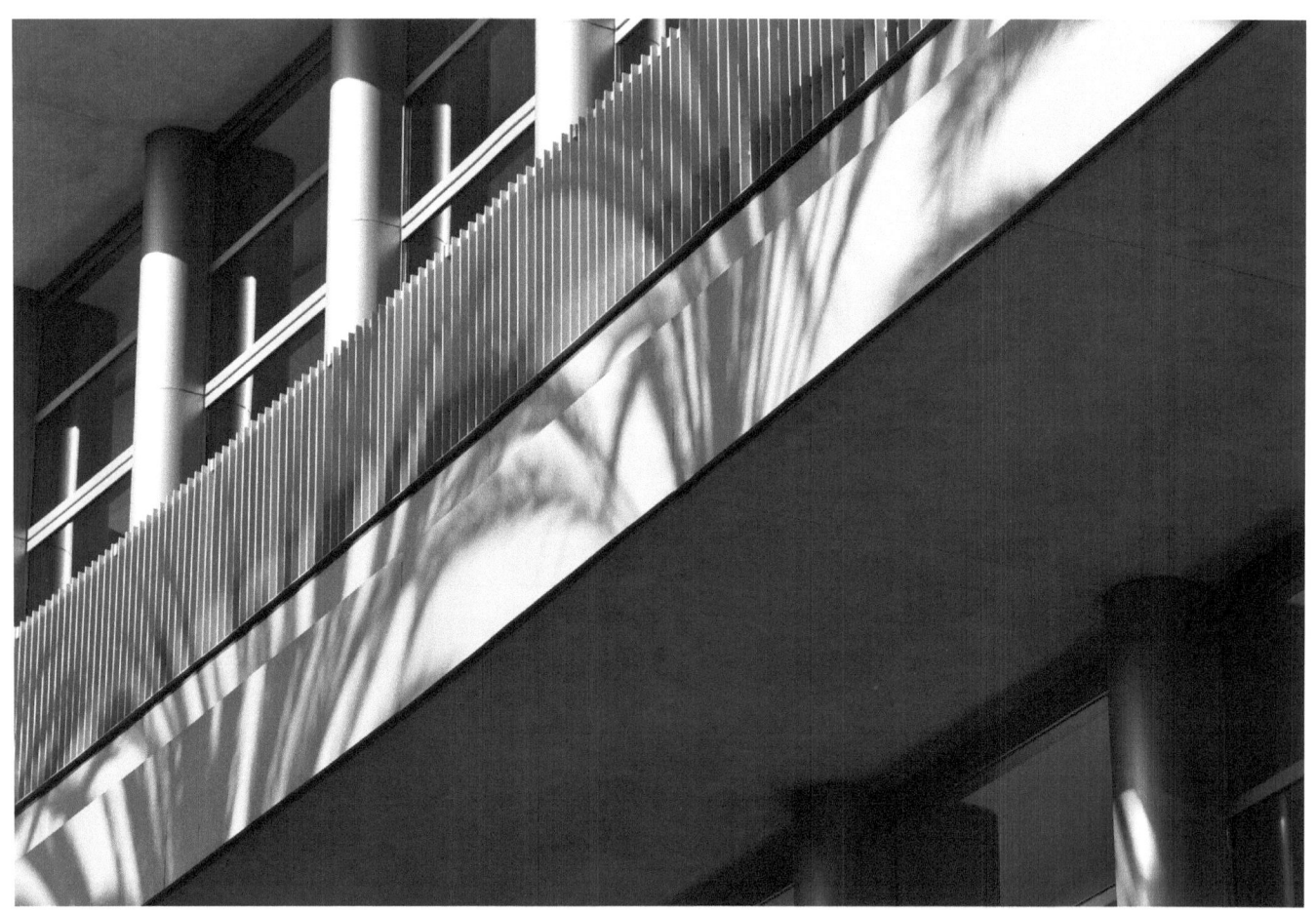

3916

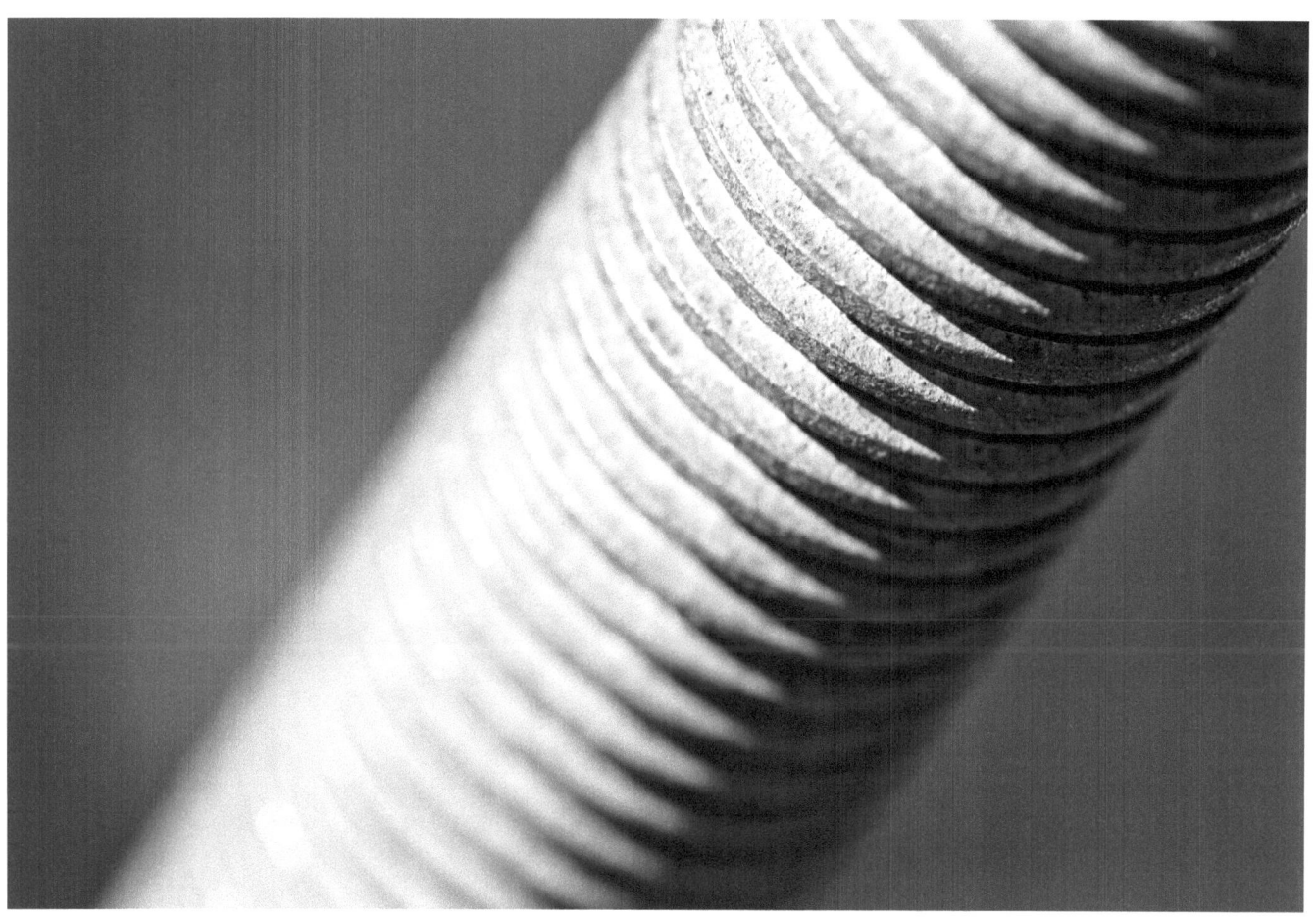

3937

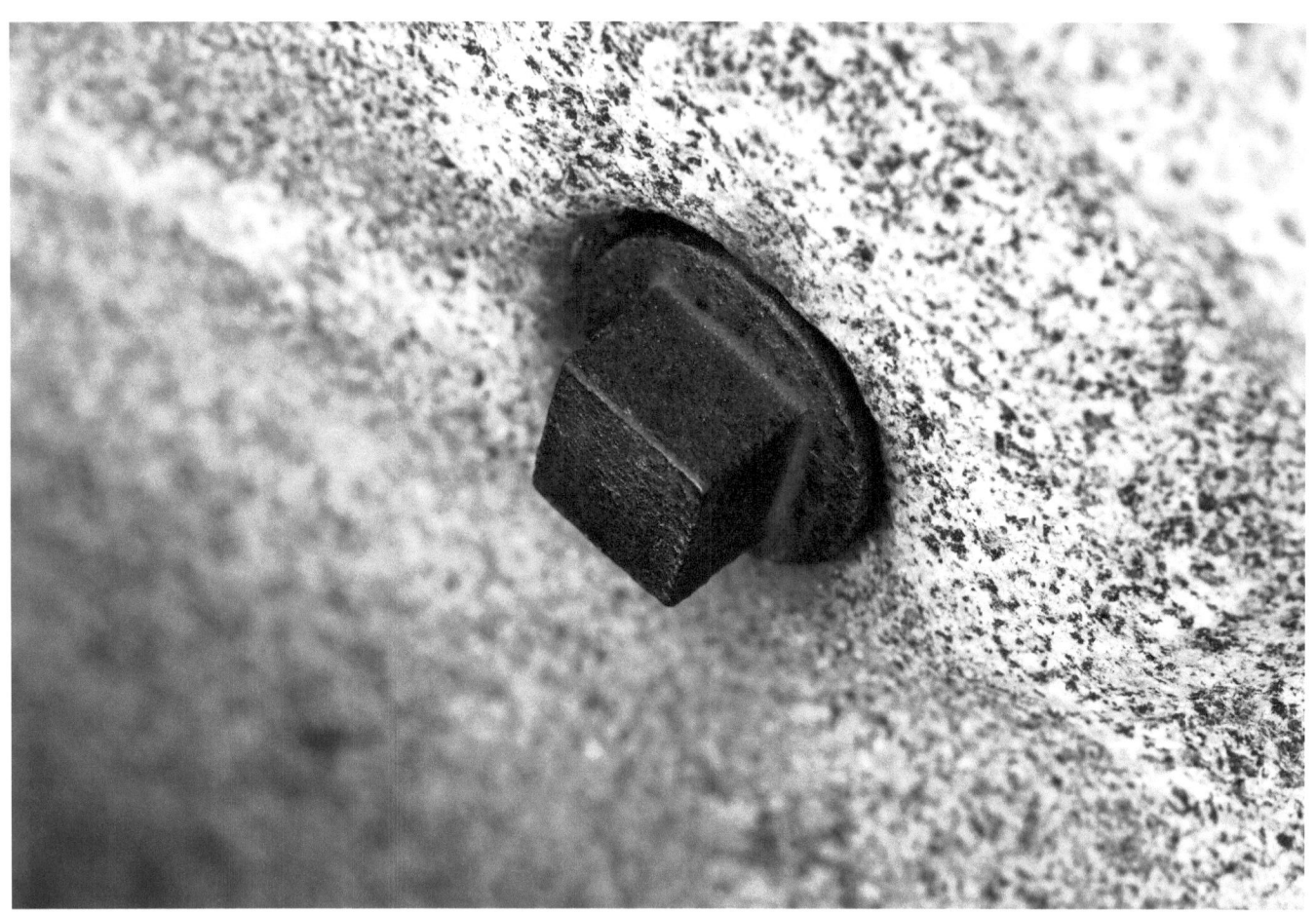

4035

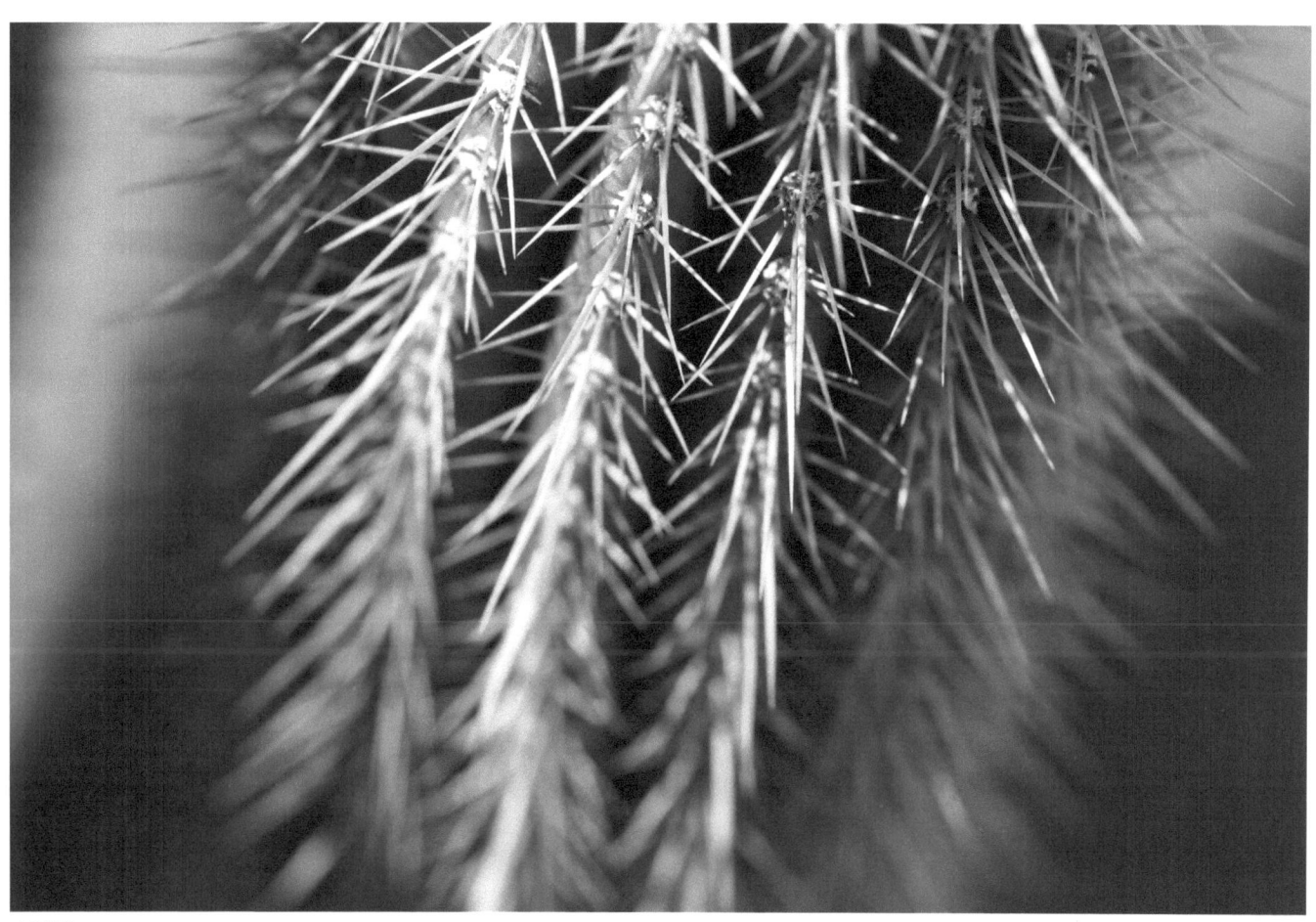

4070

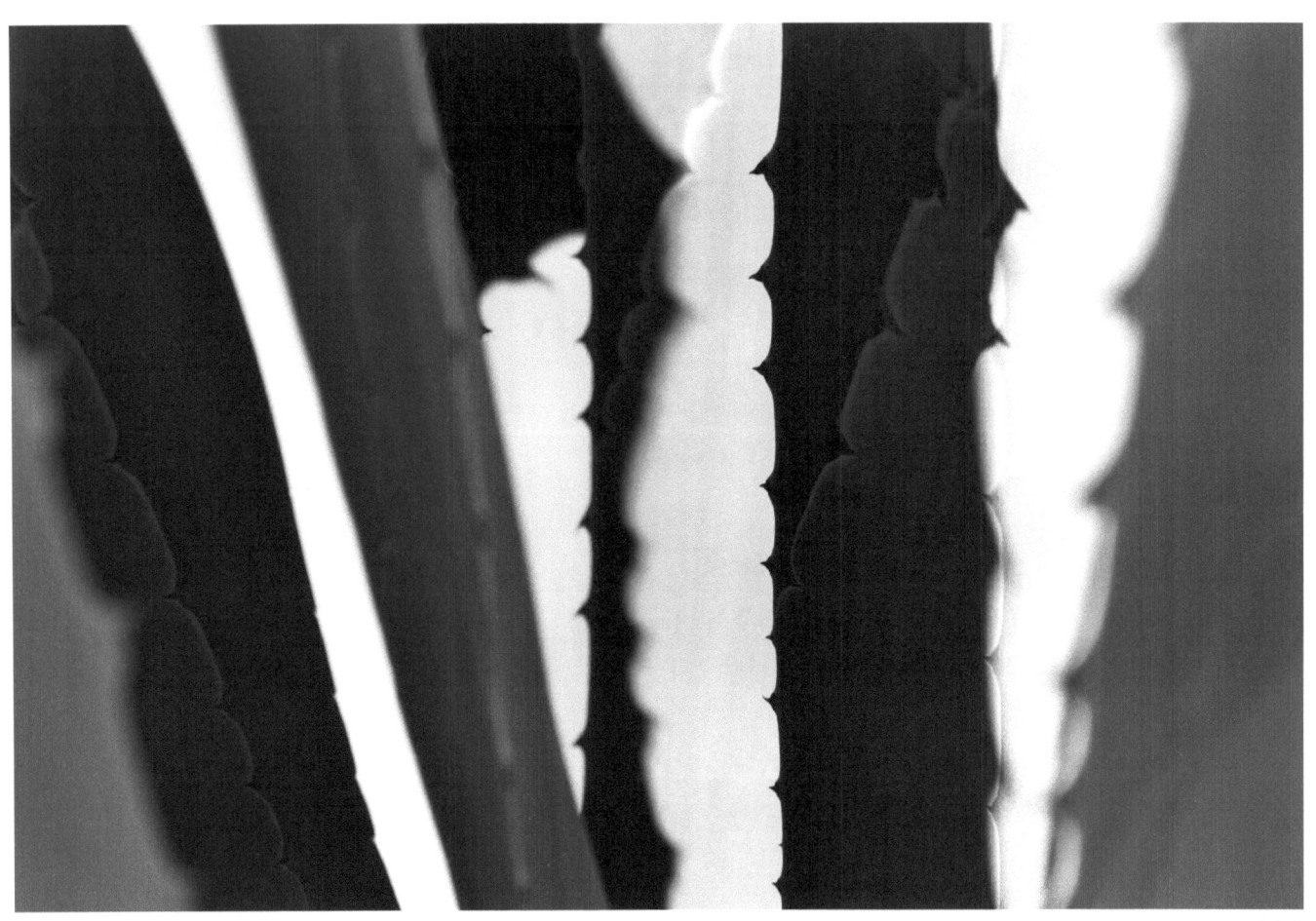

4099

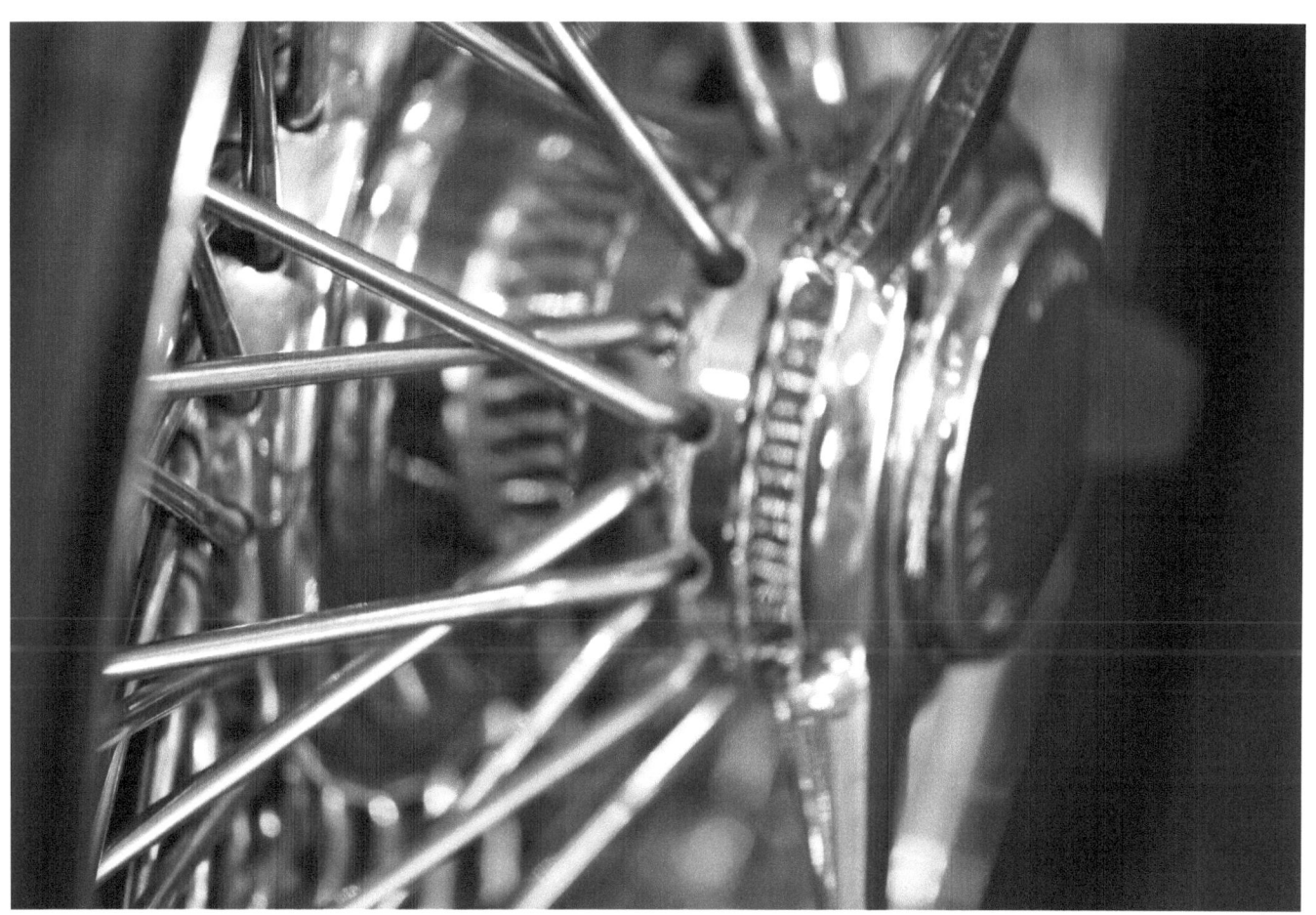

4193

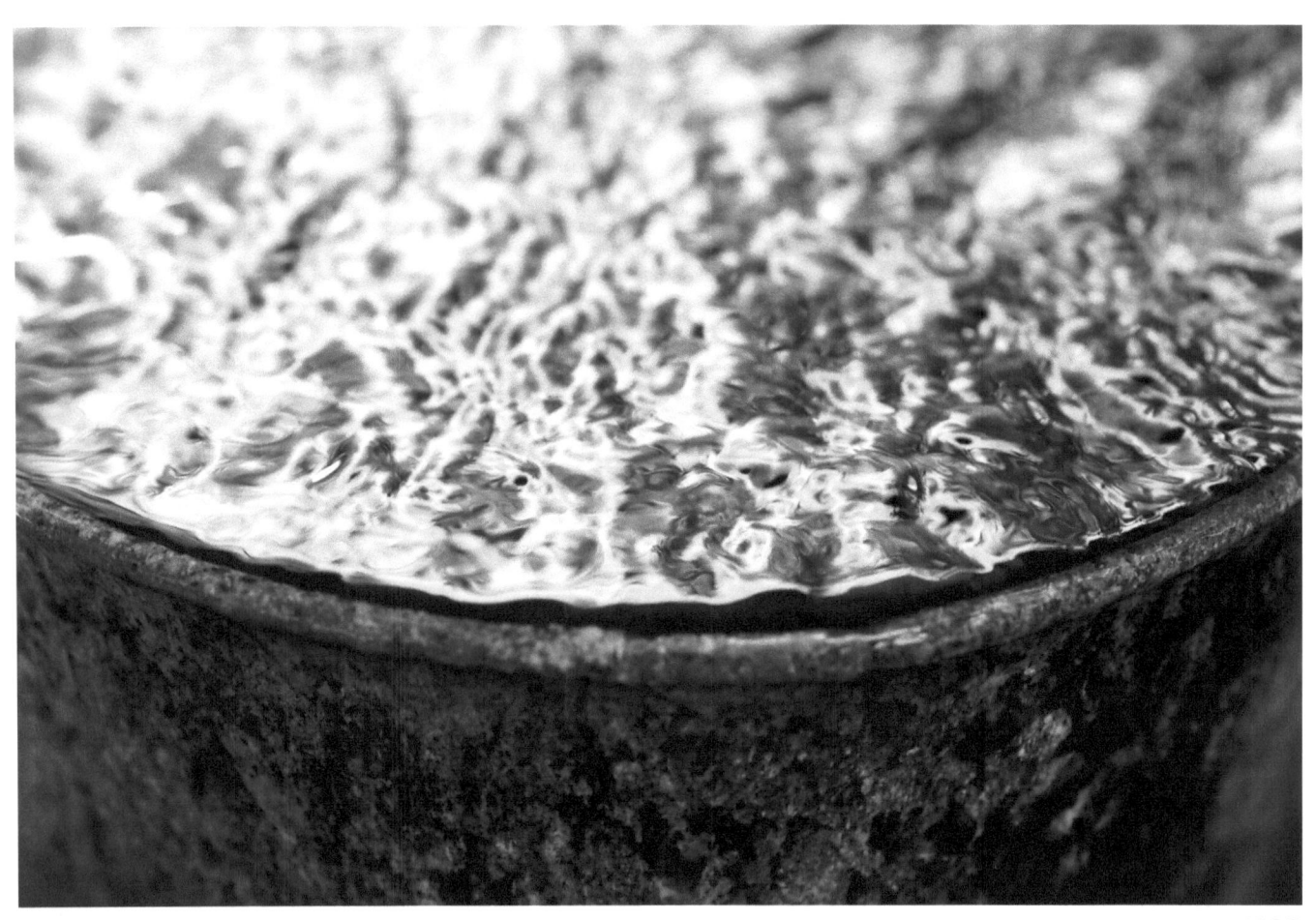

4533

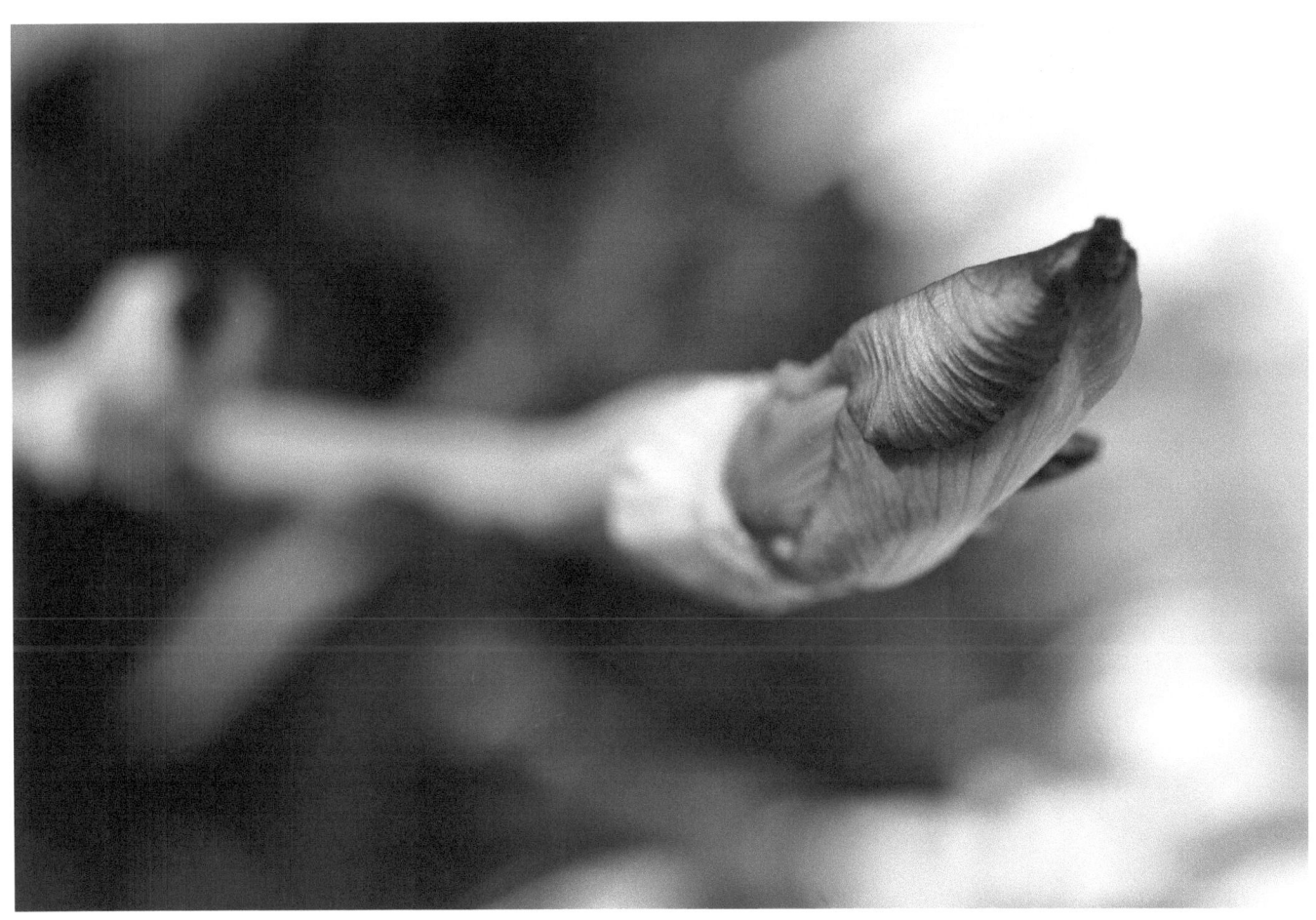

5492

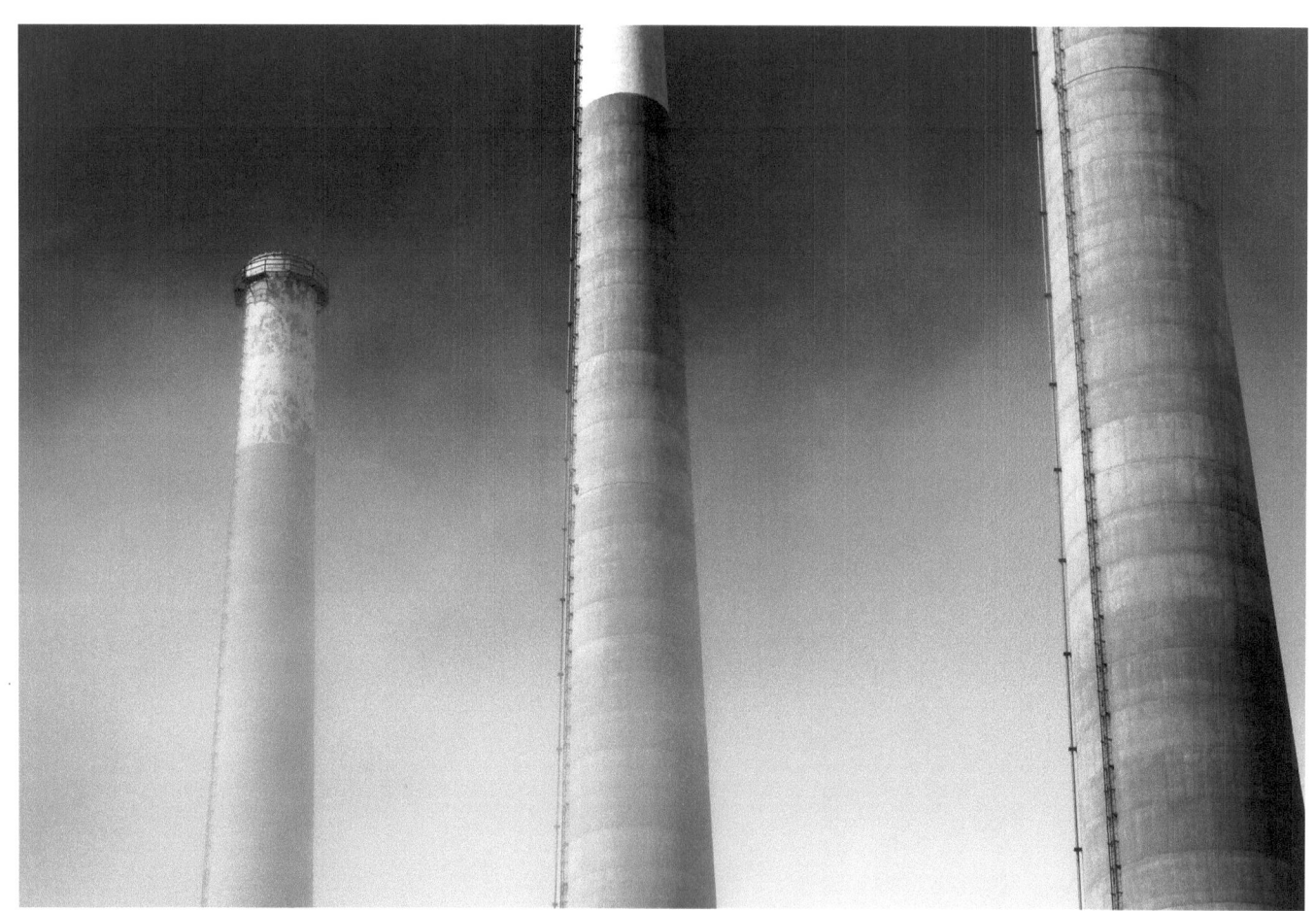

5541

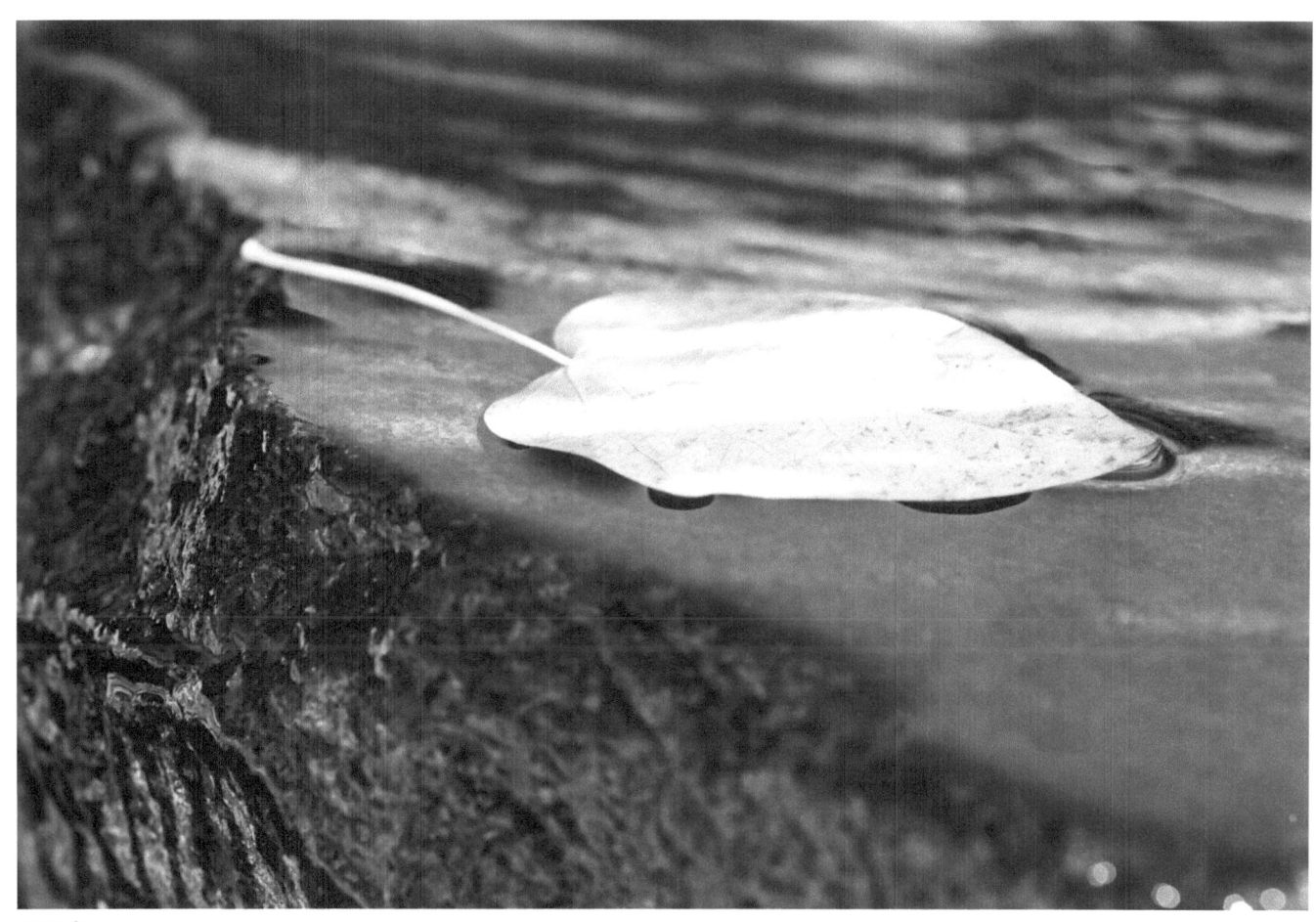

5750

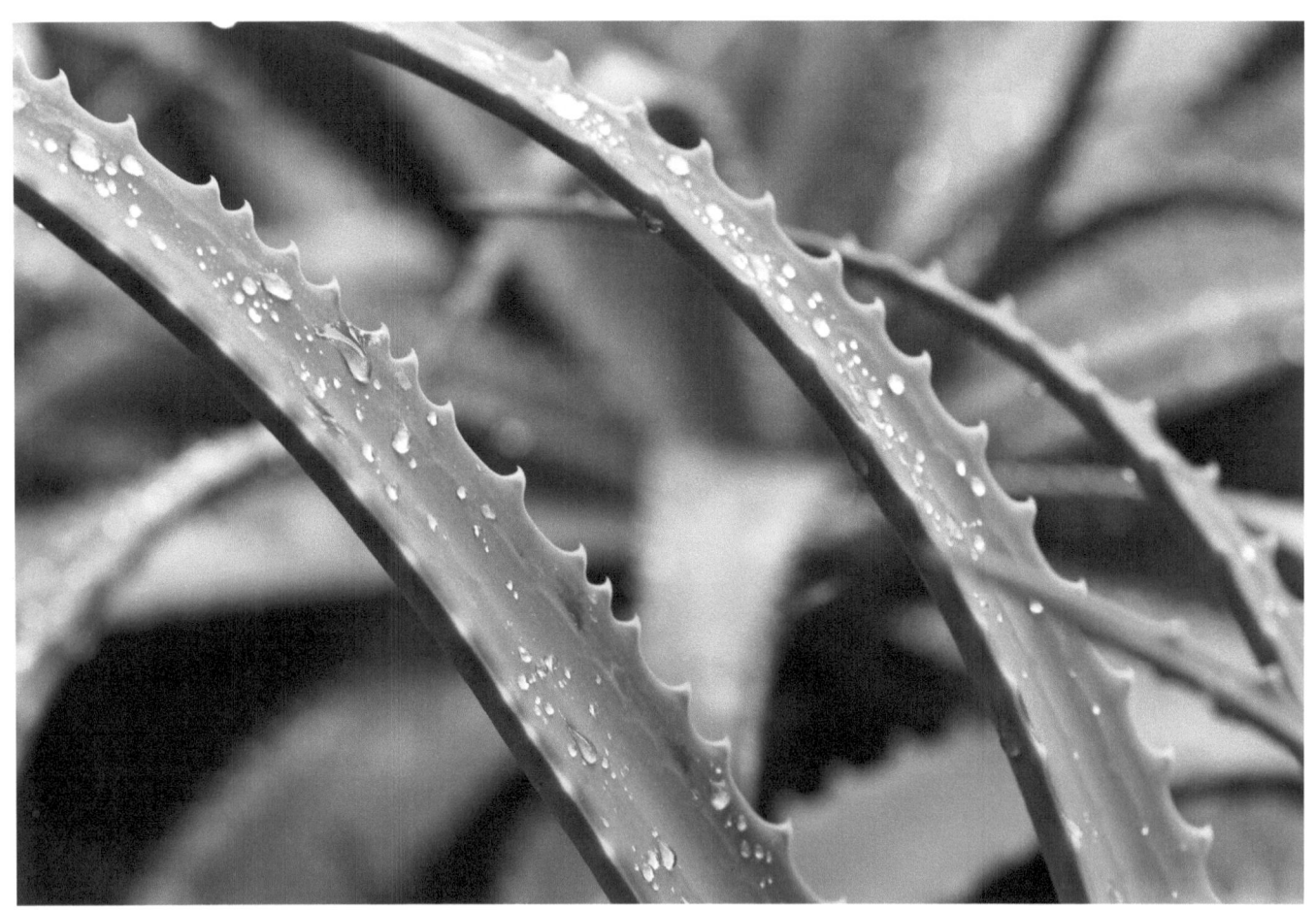

5784

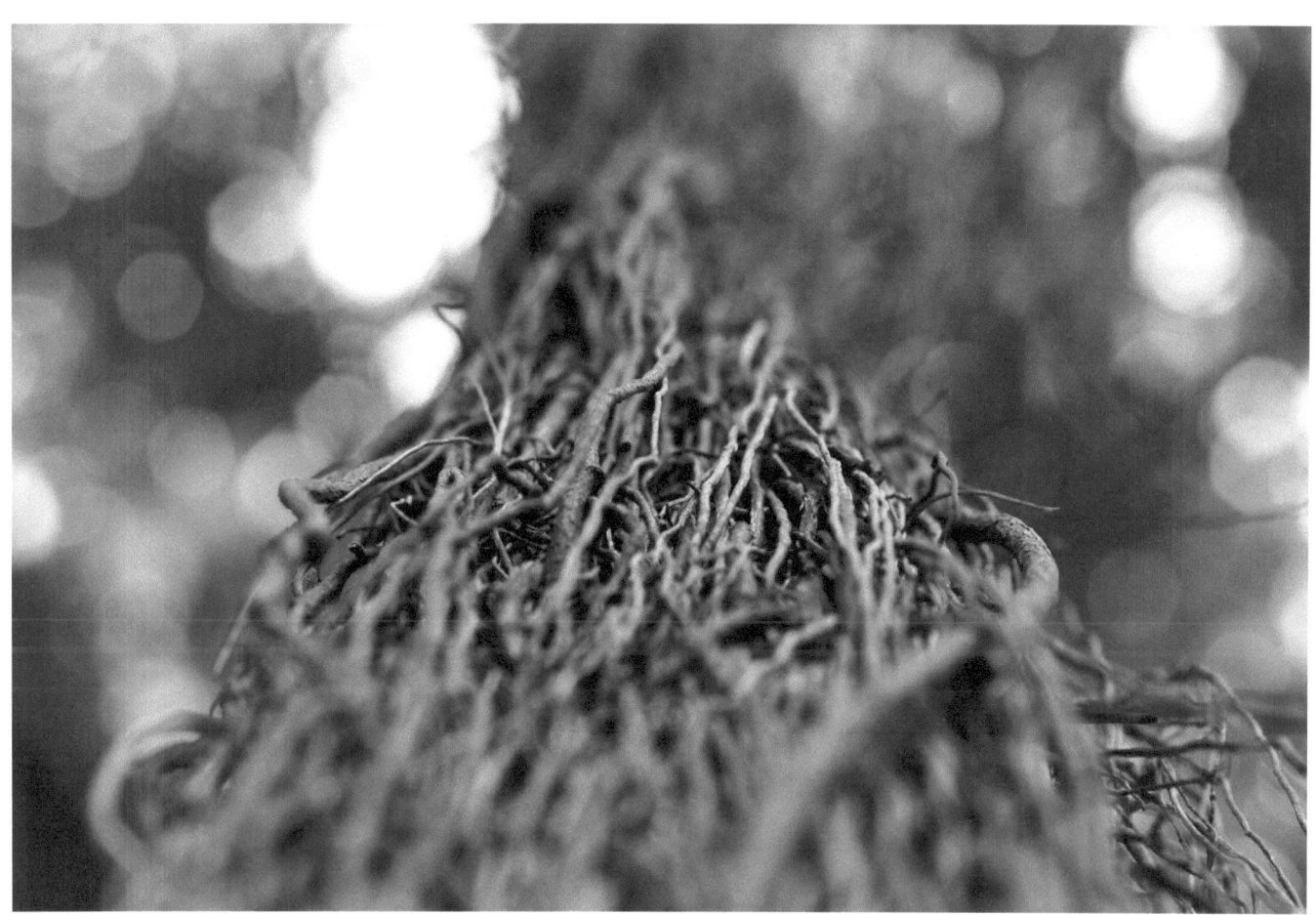

5811

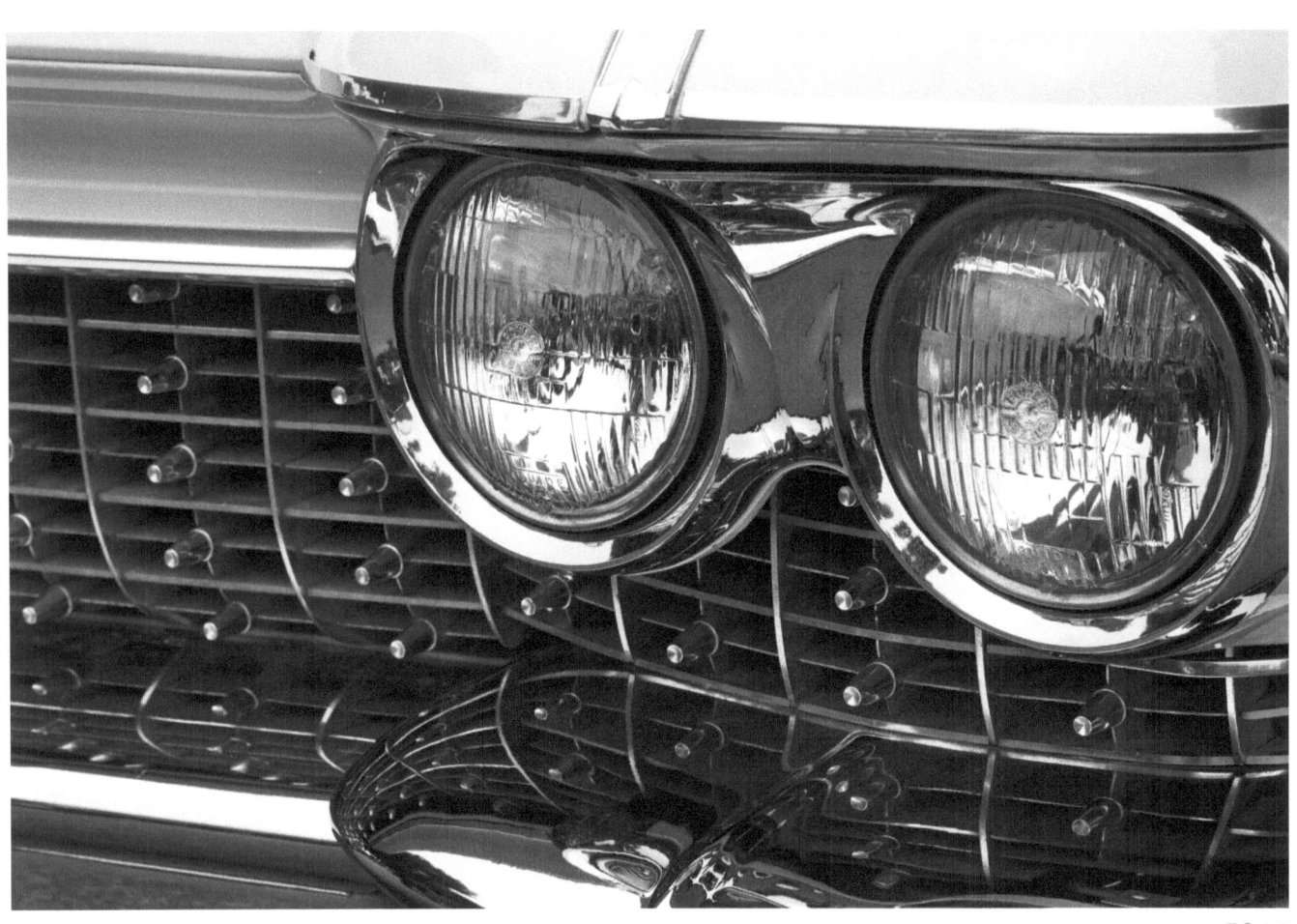

5844

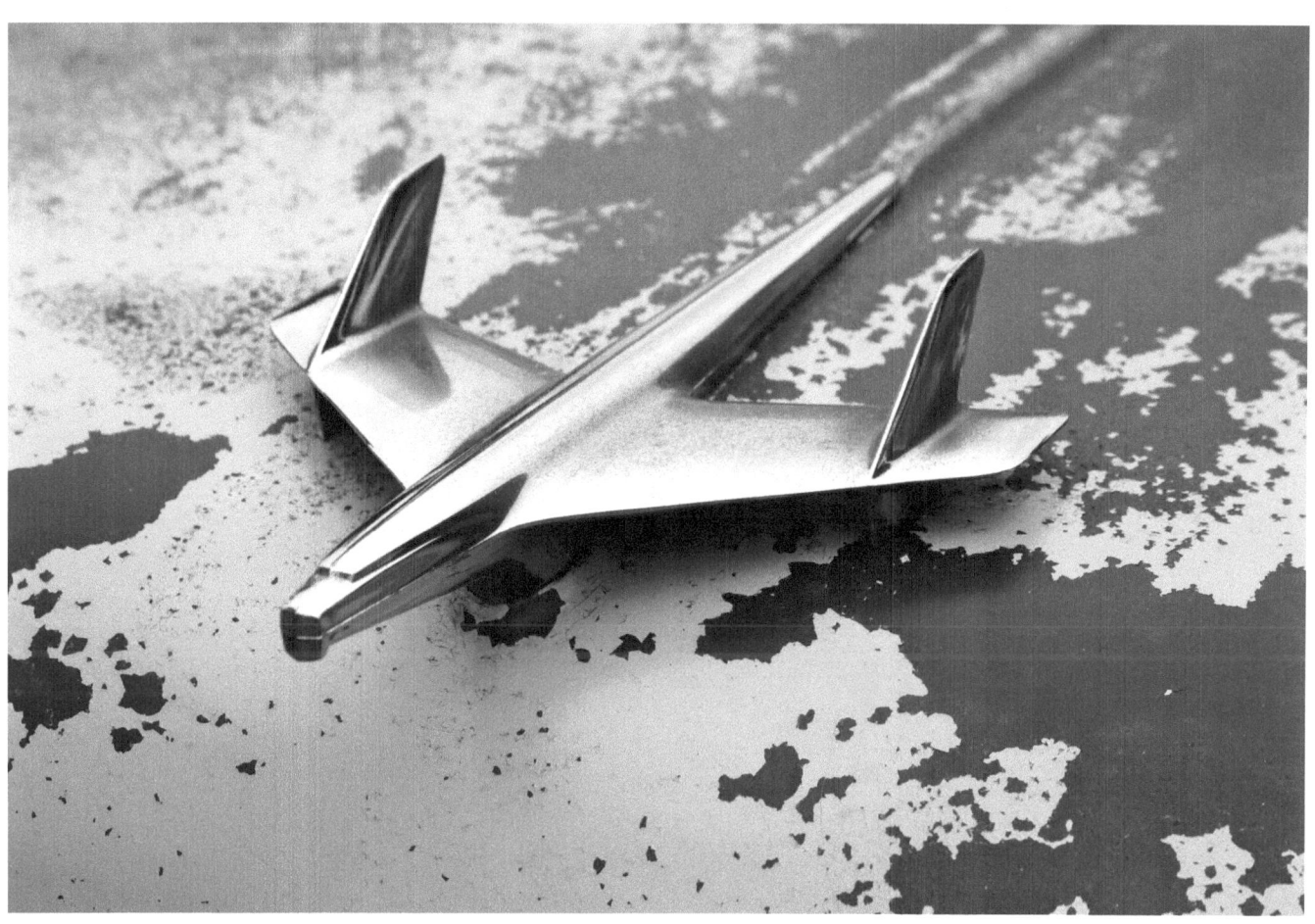

5846

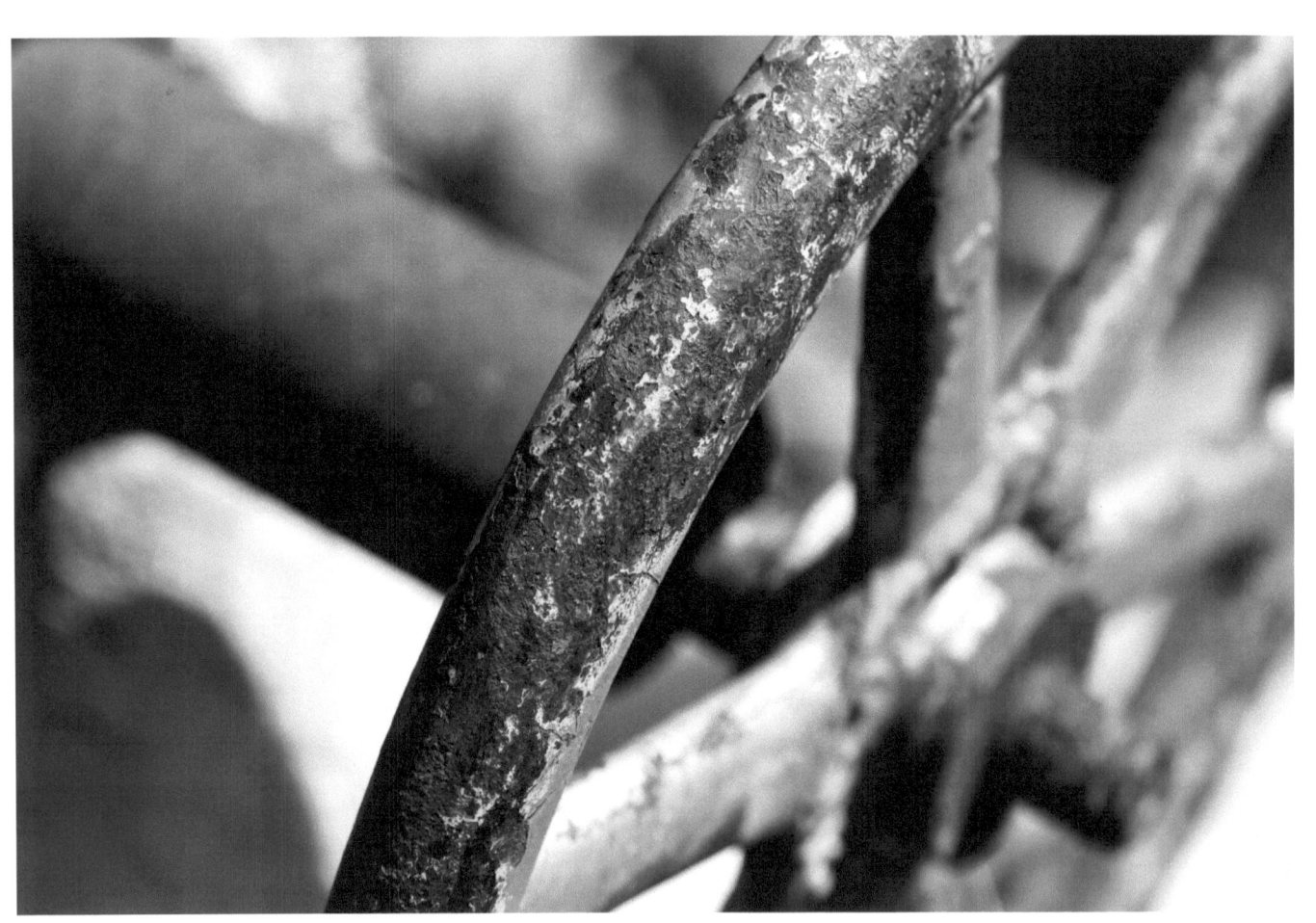

6095

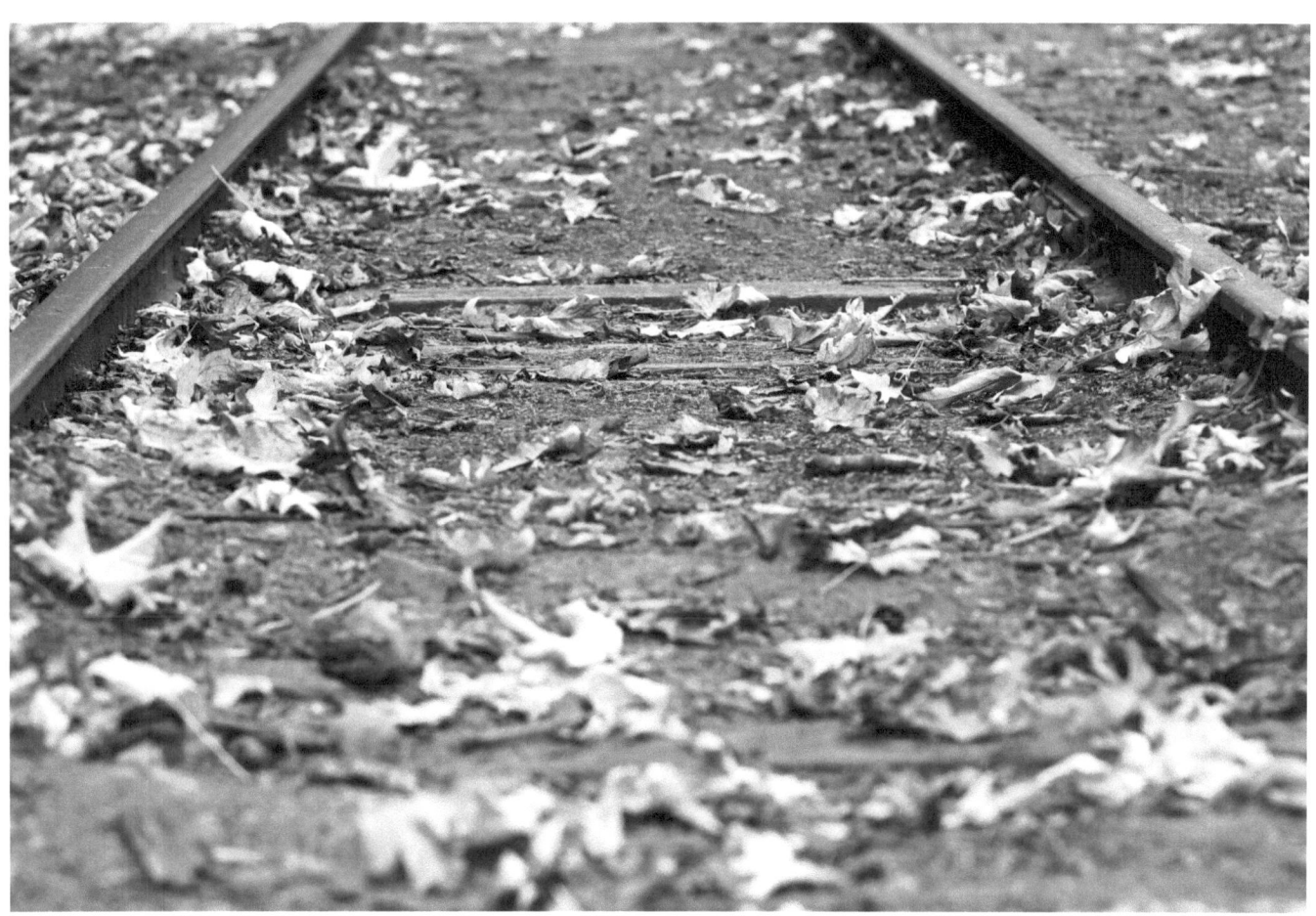

6176

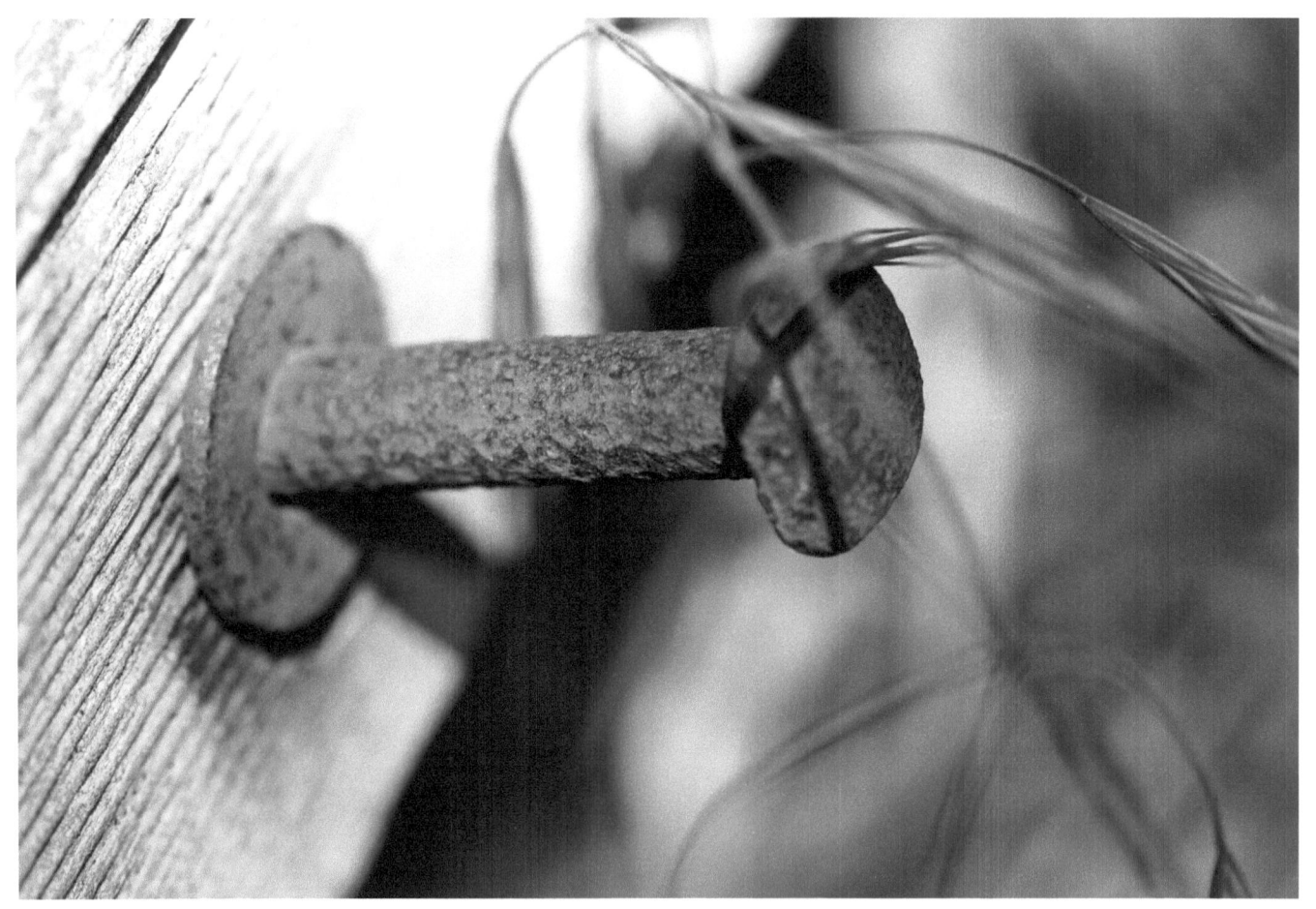

7182

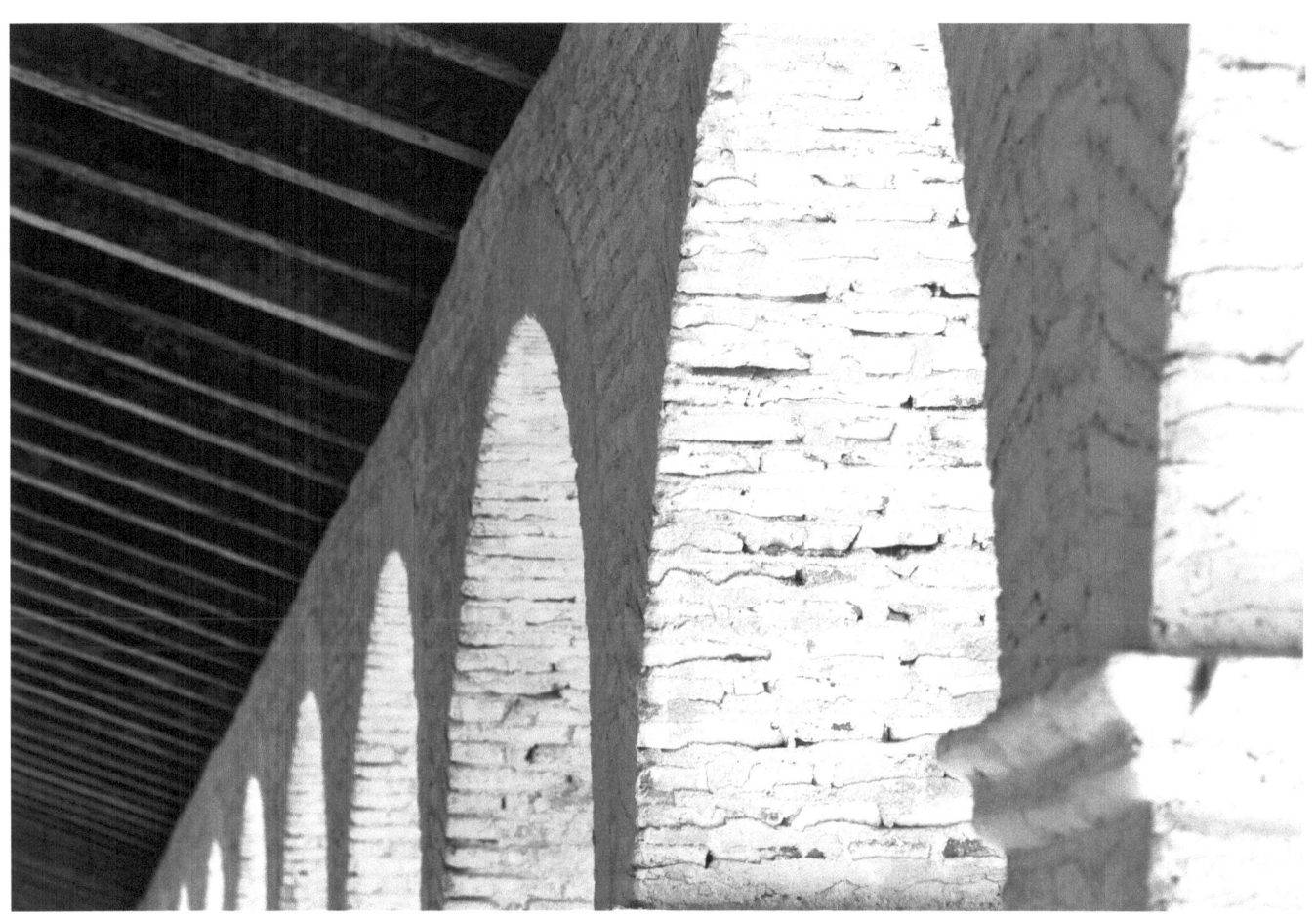

7656

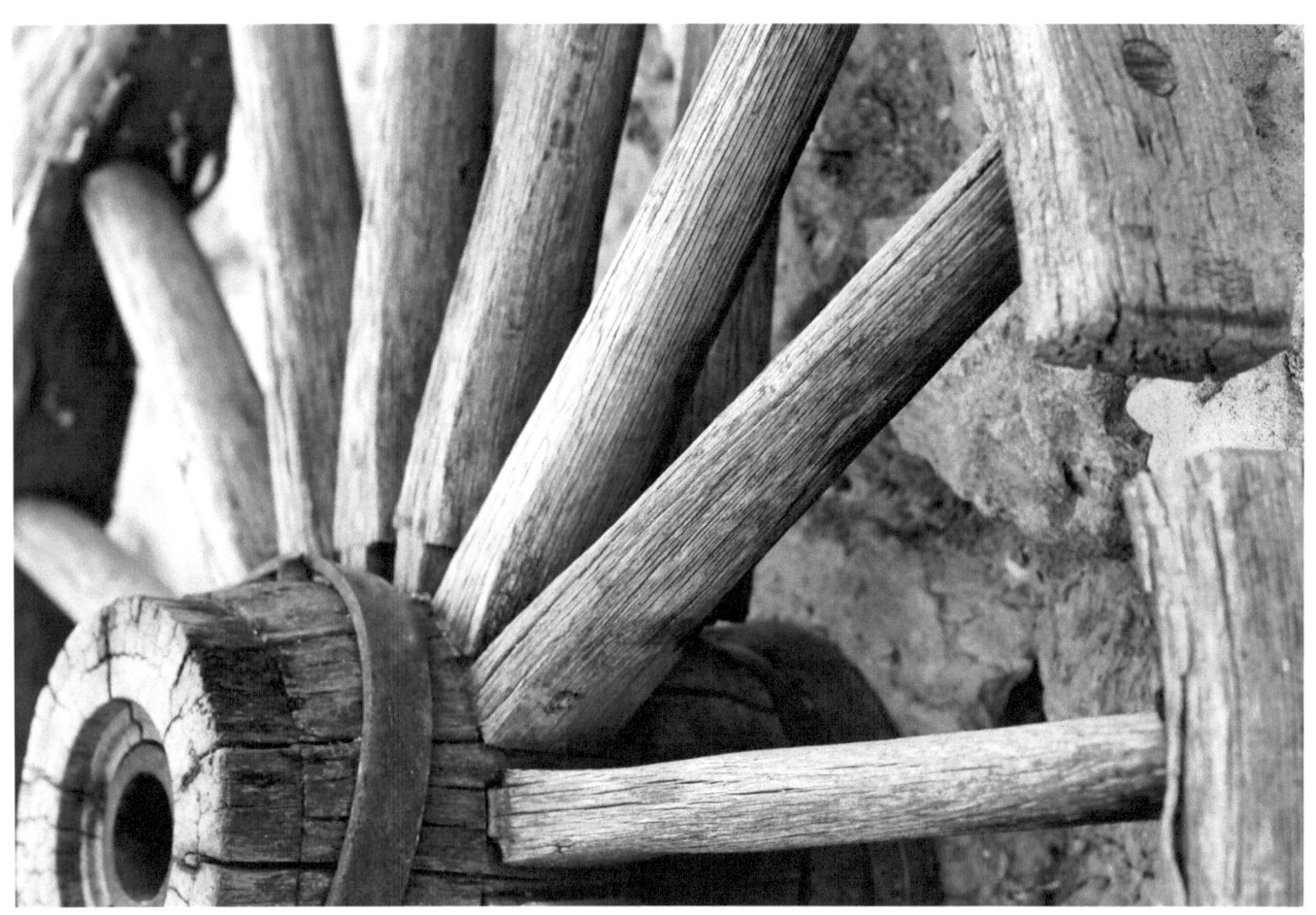

7783

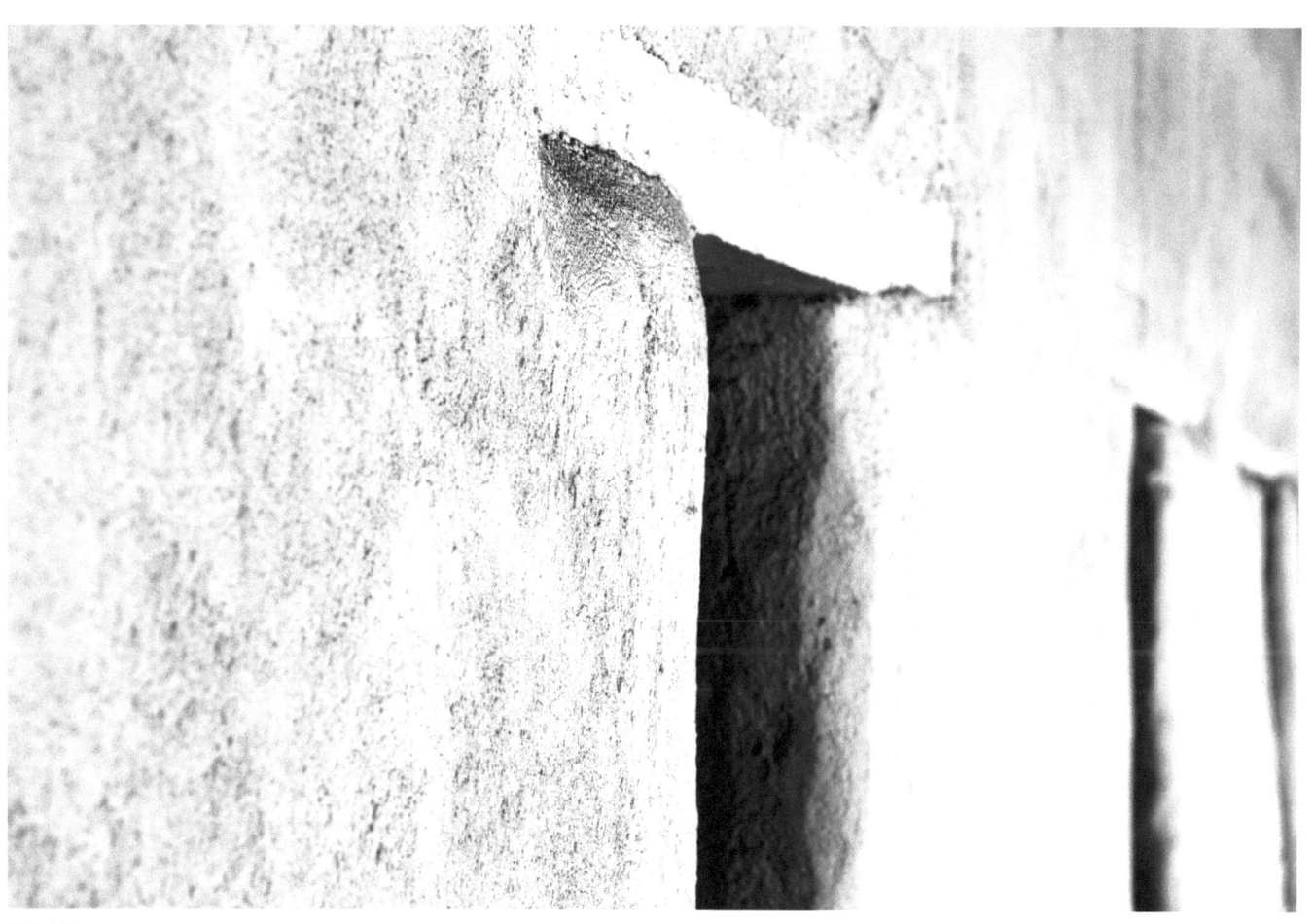

7843

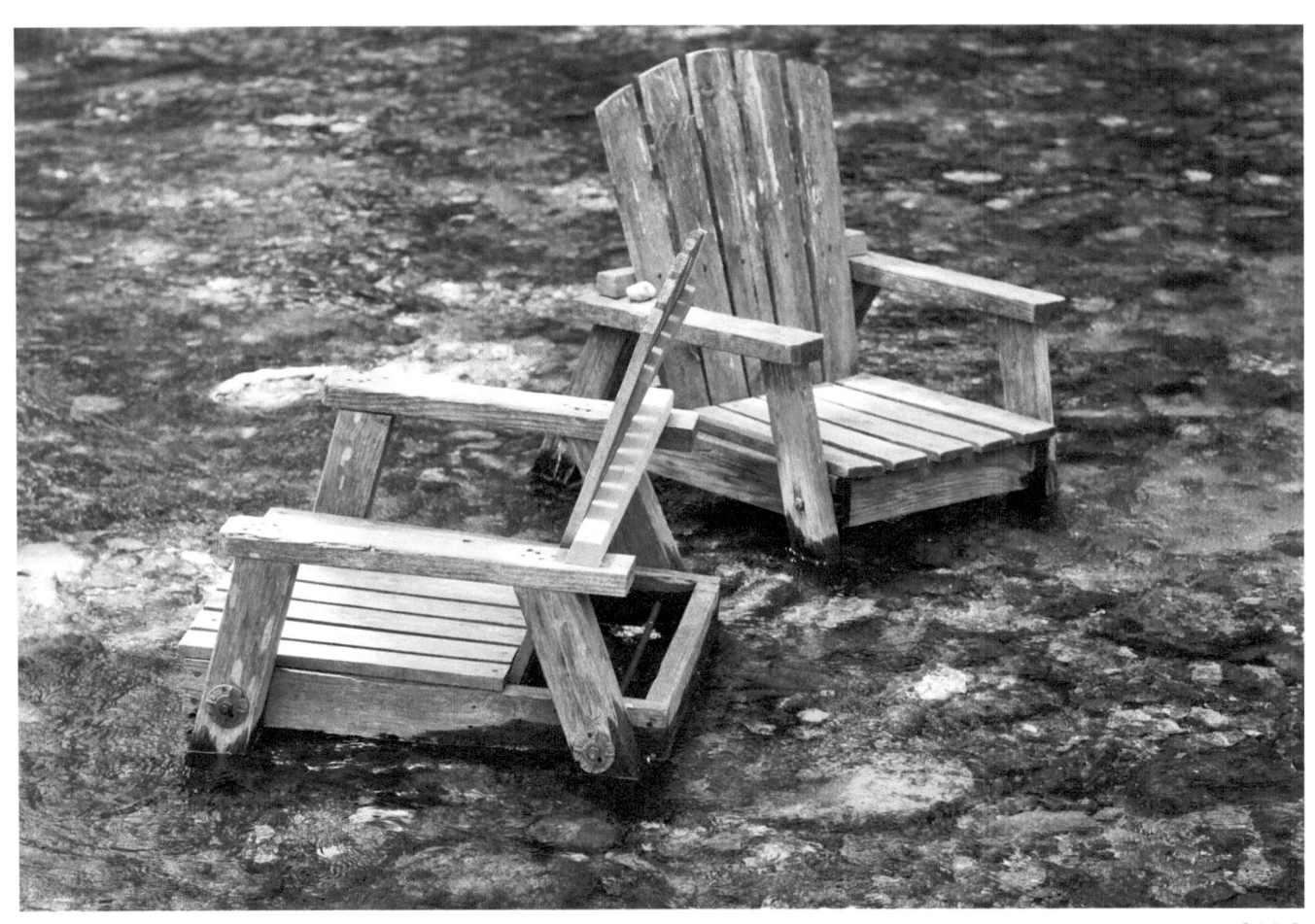

8173

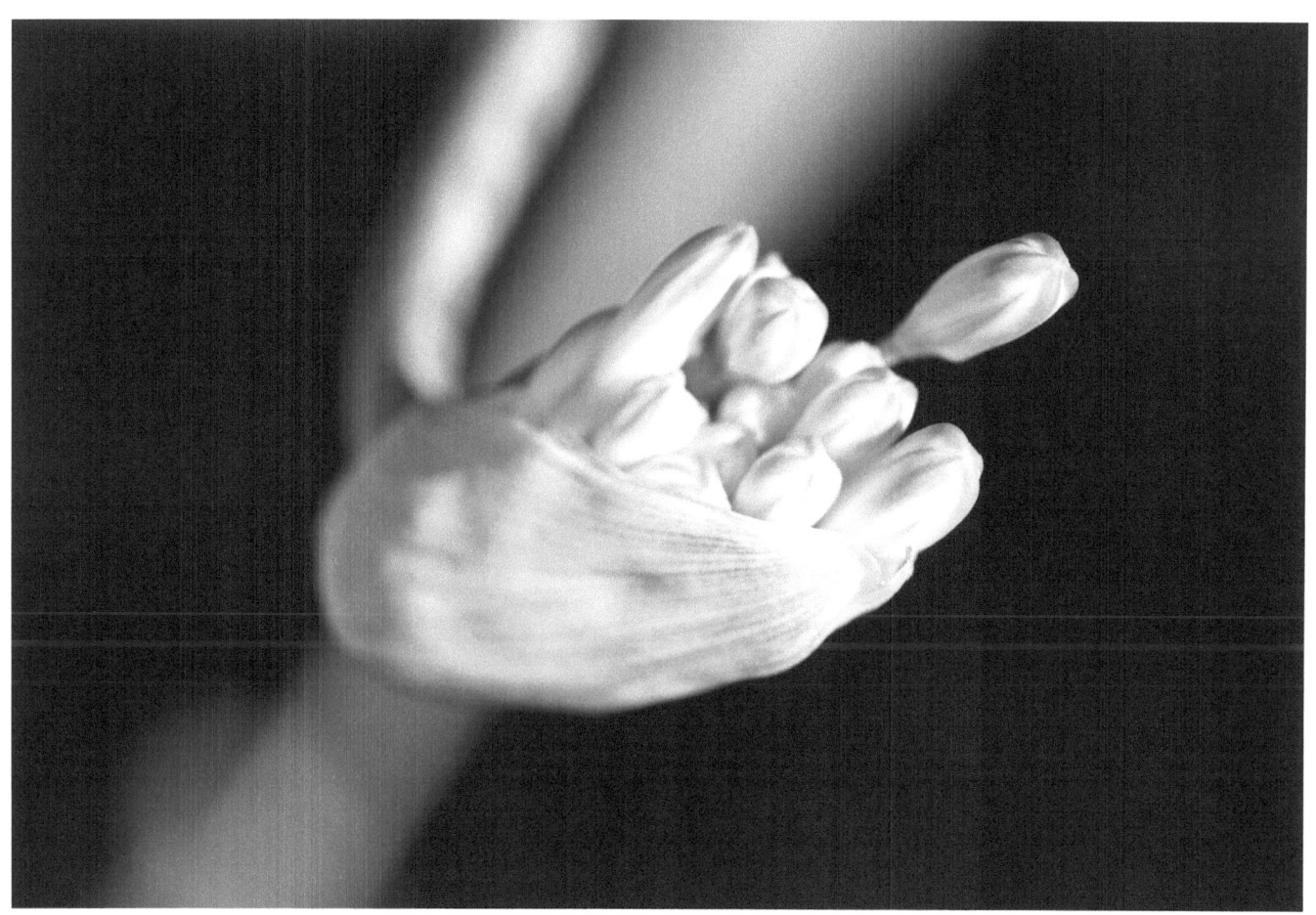

8407

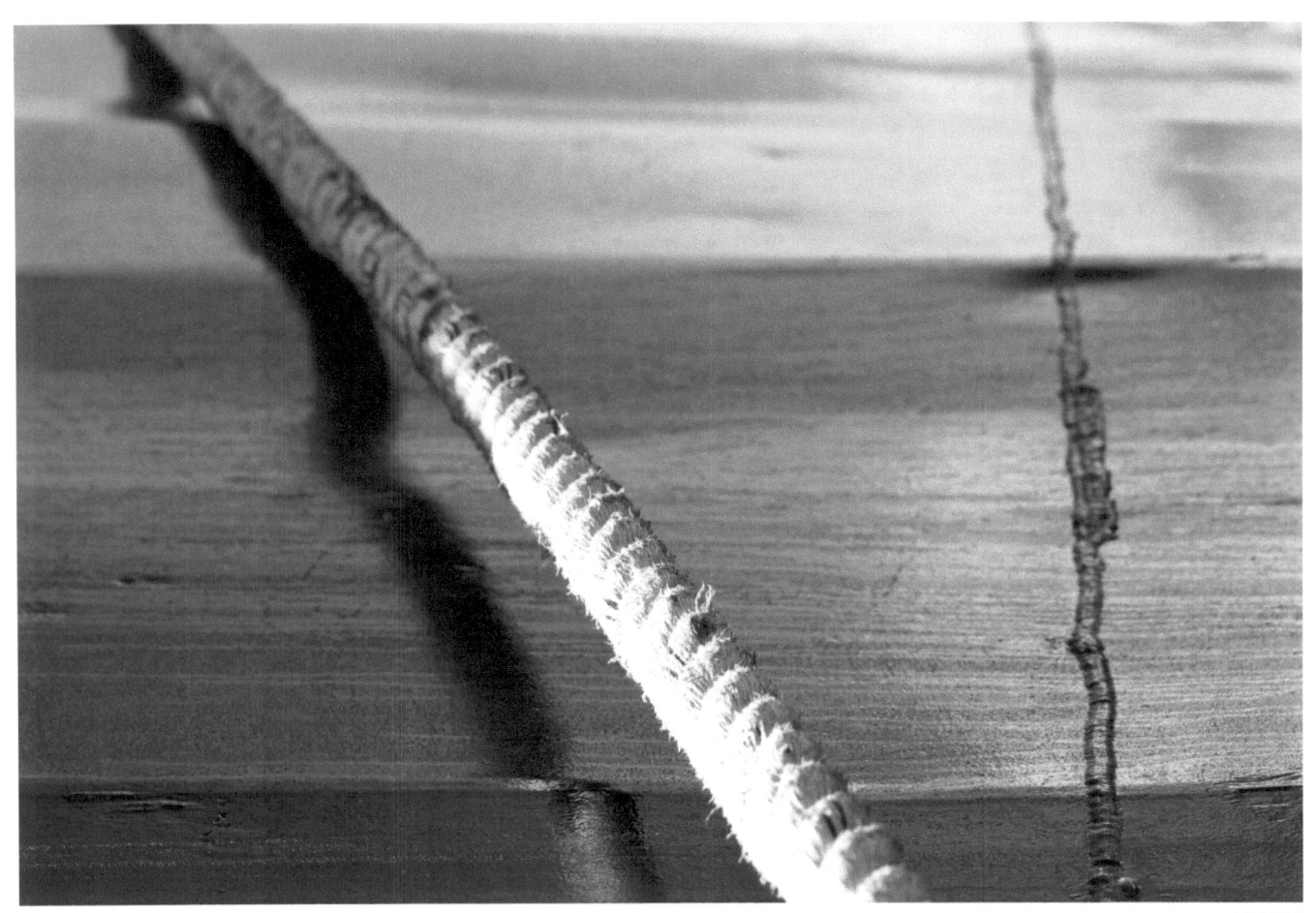

8470

8471

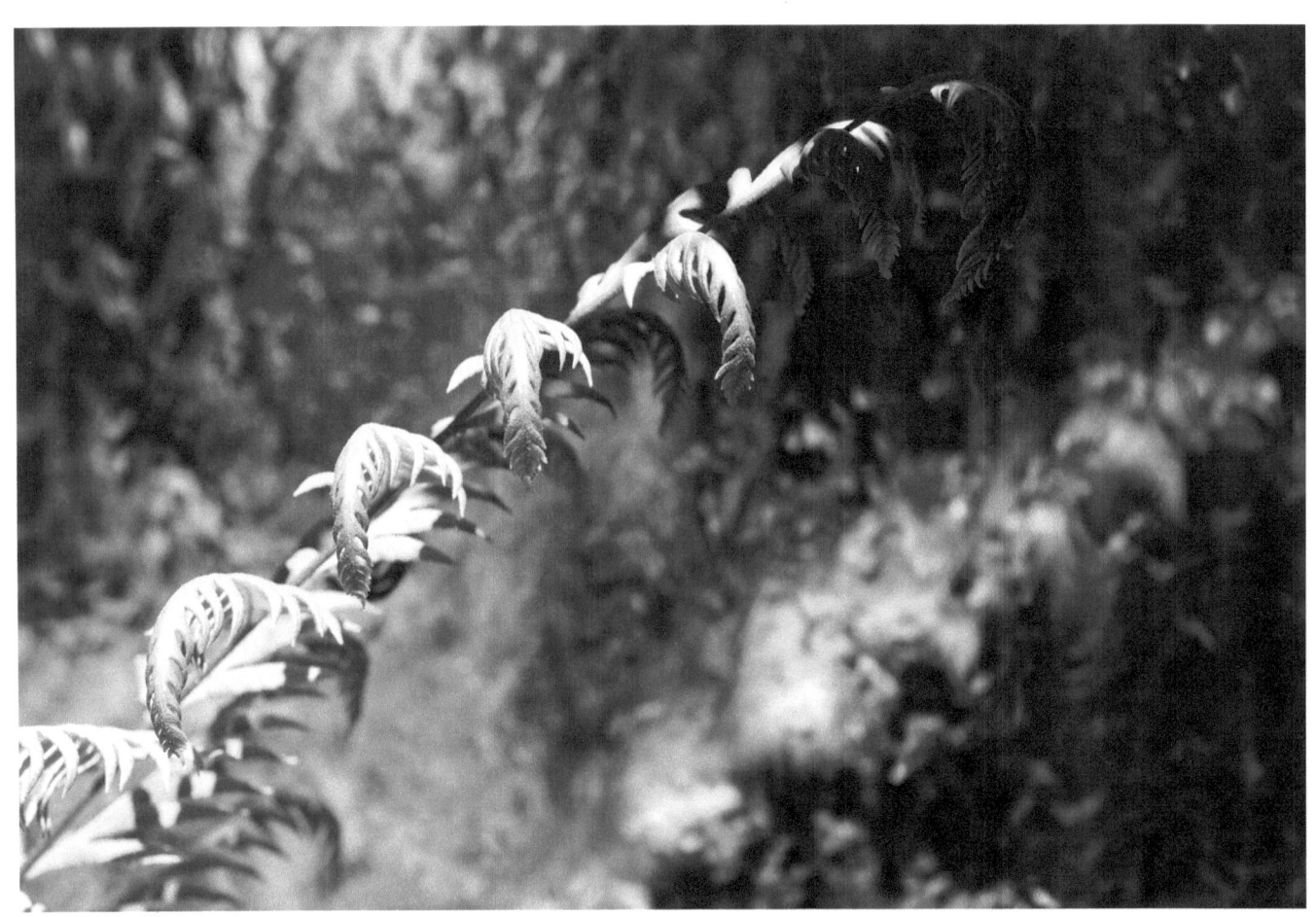

8889

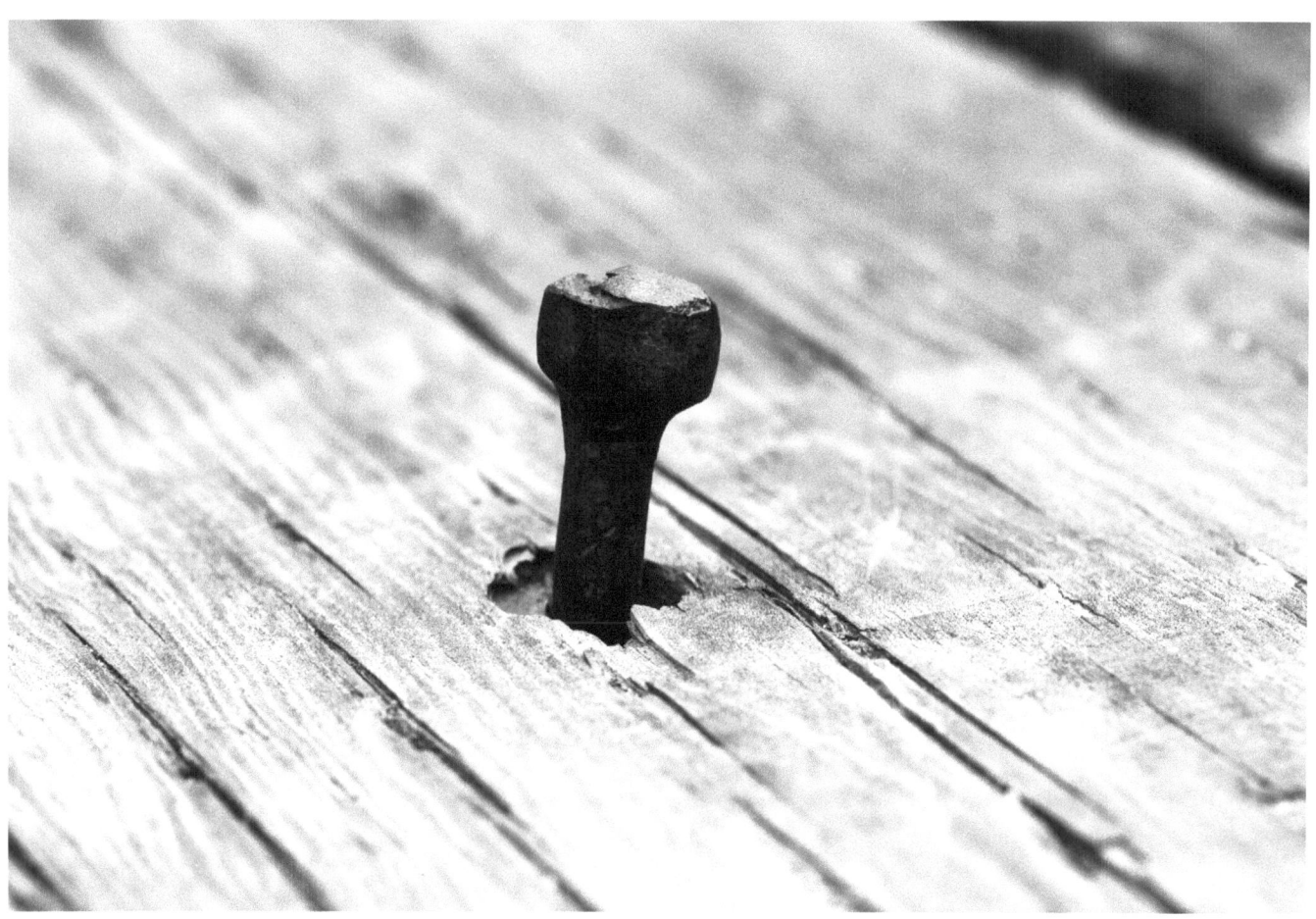

9024

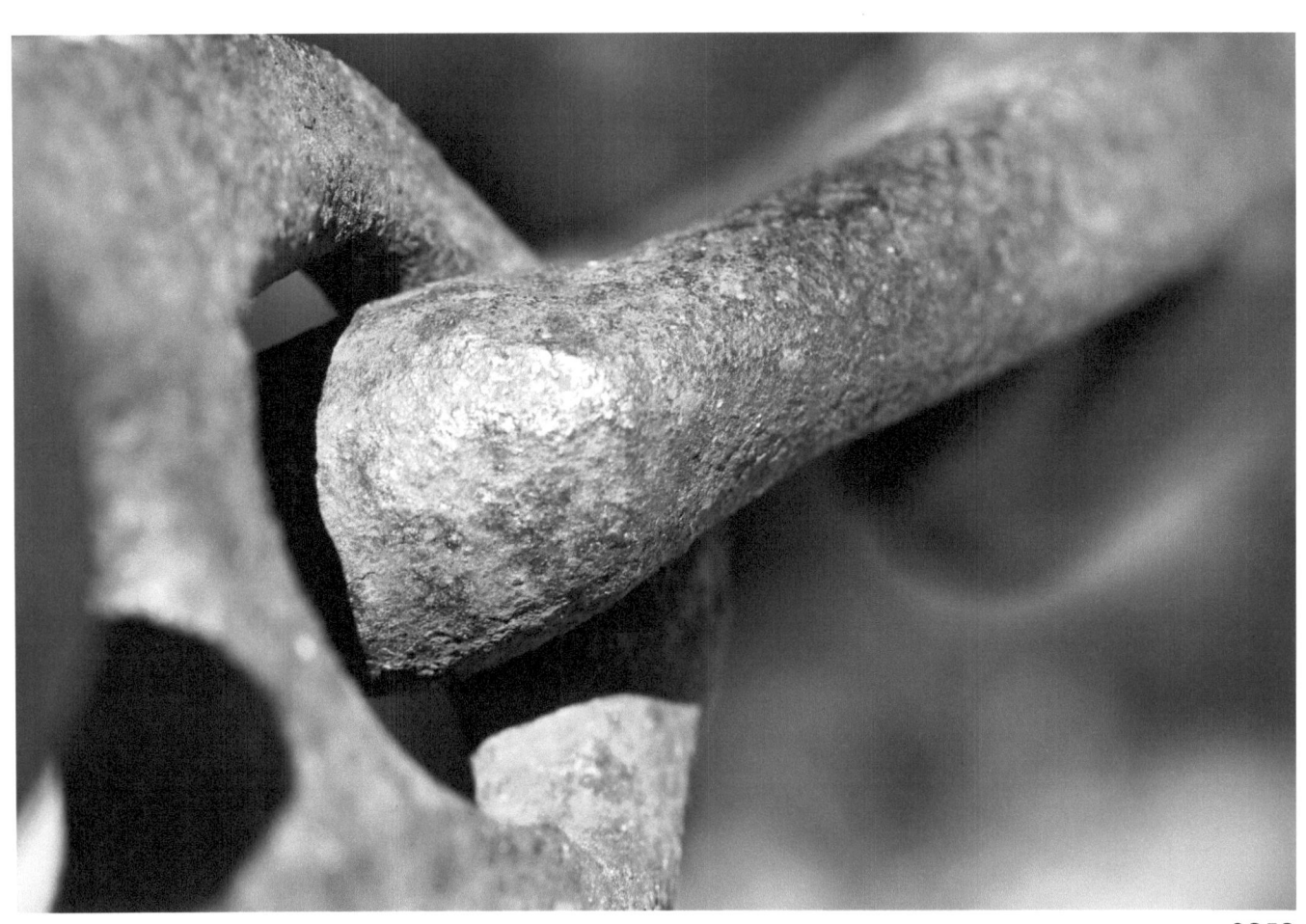

9353

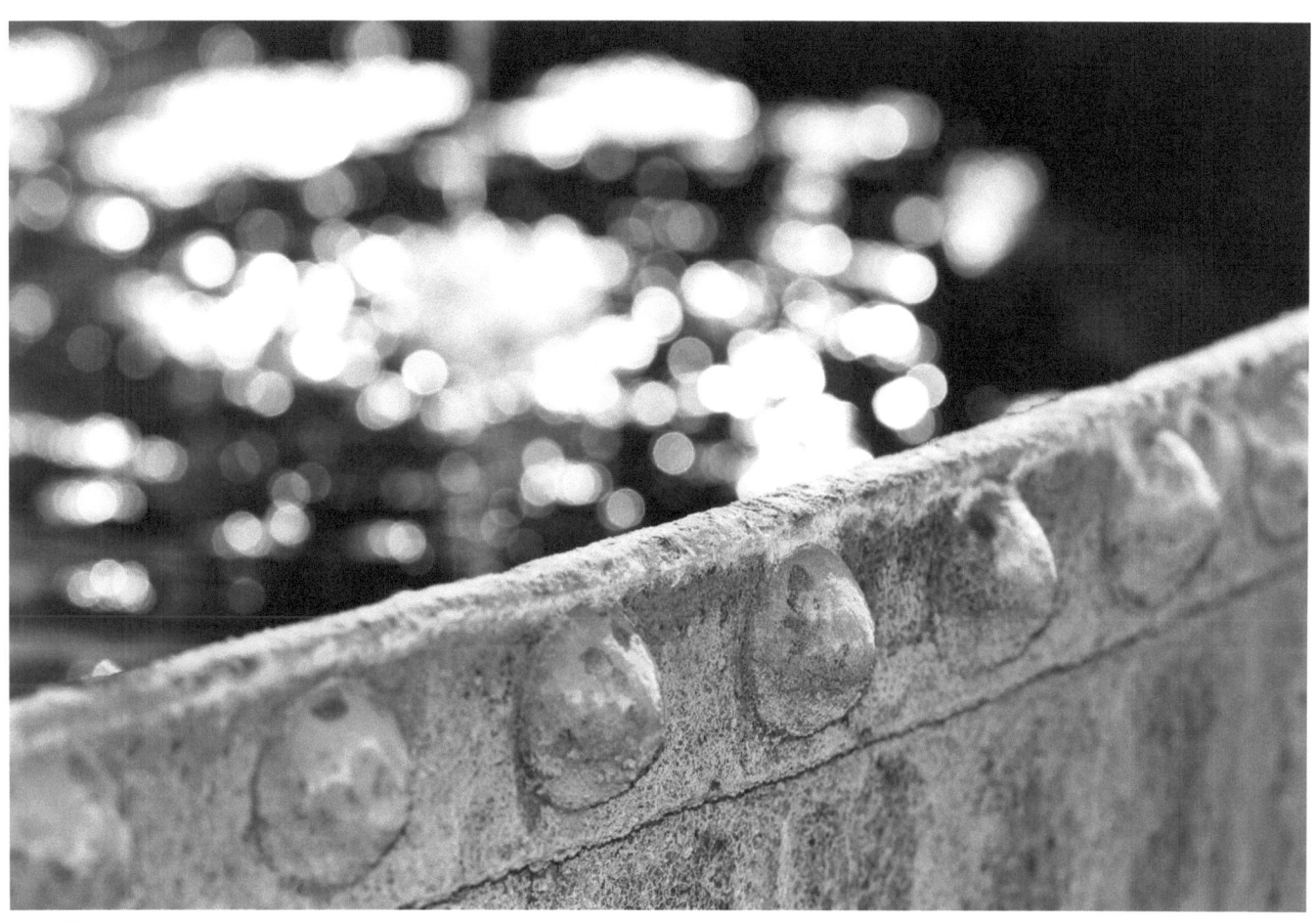

9430

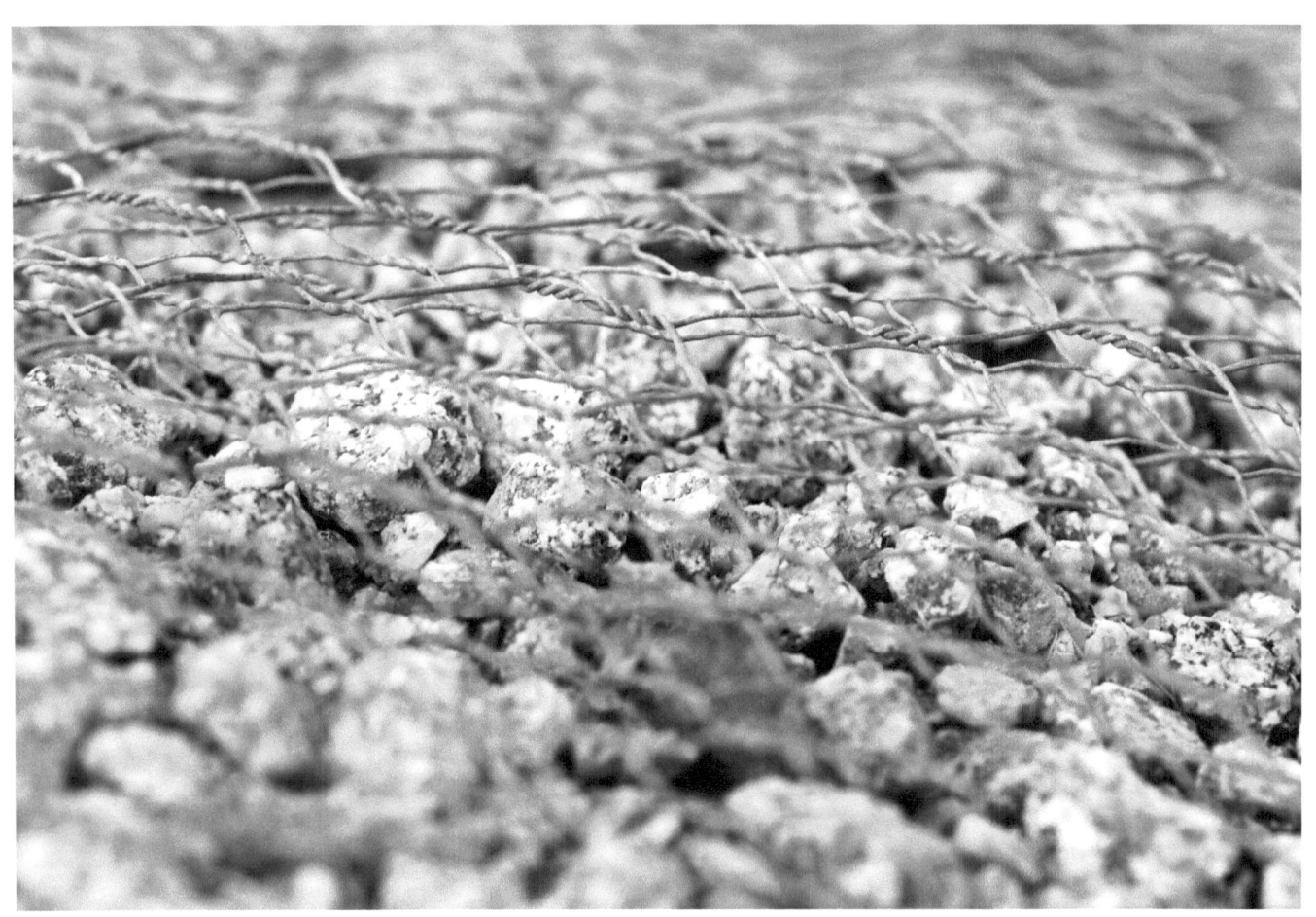

9970

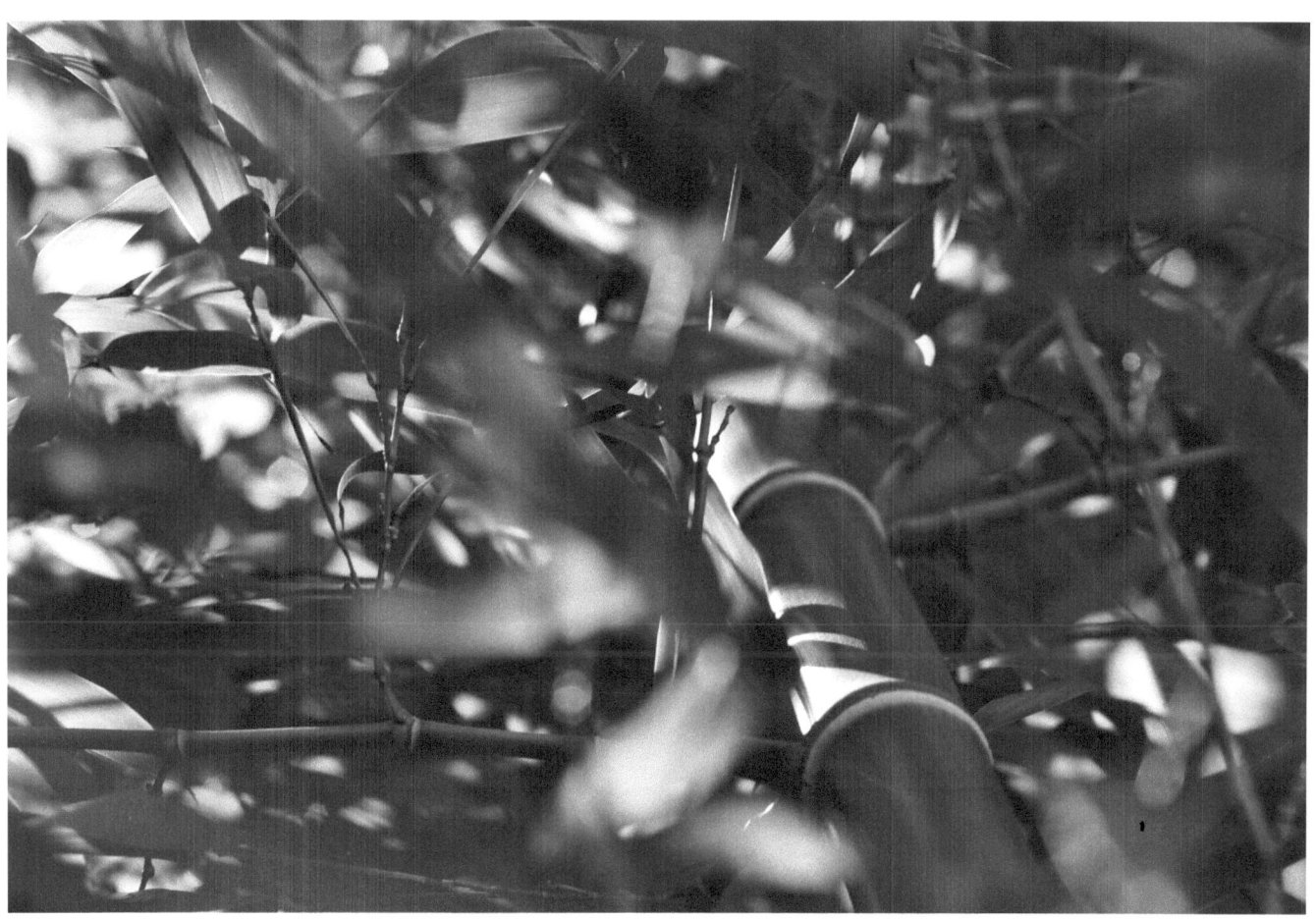

9975

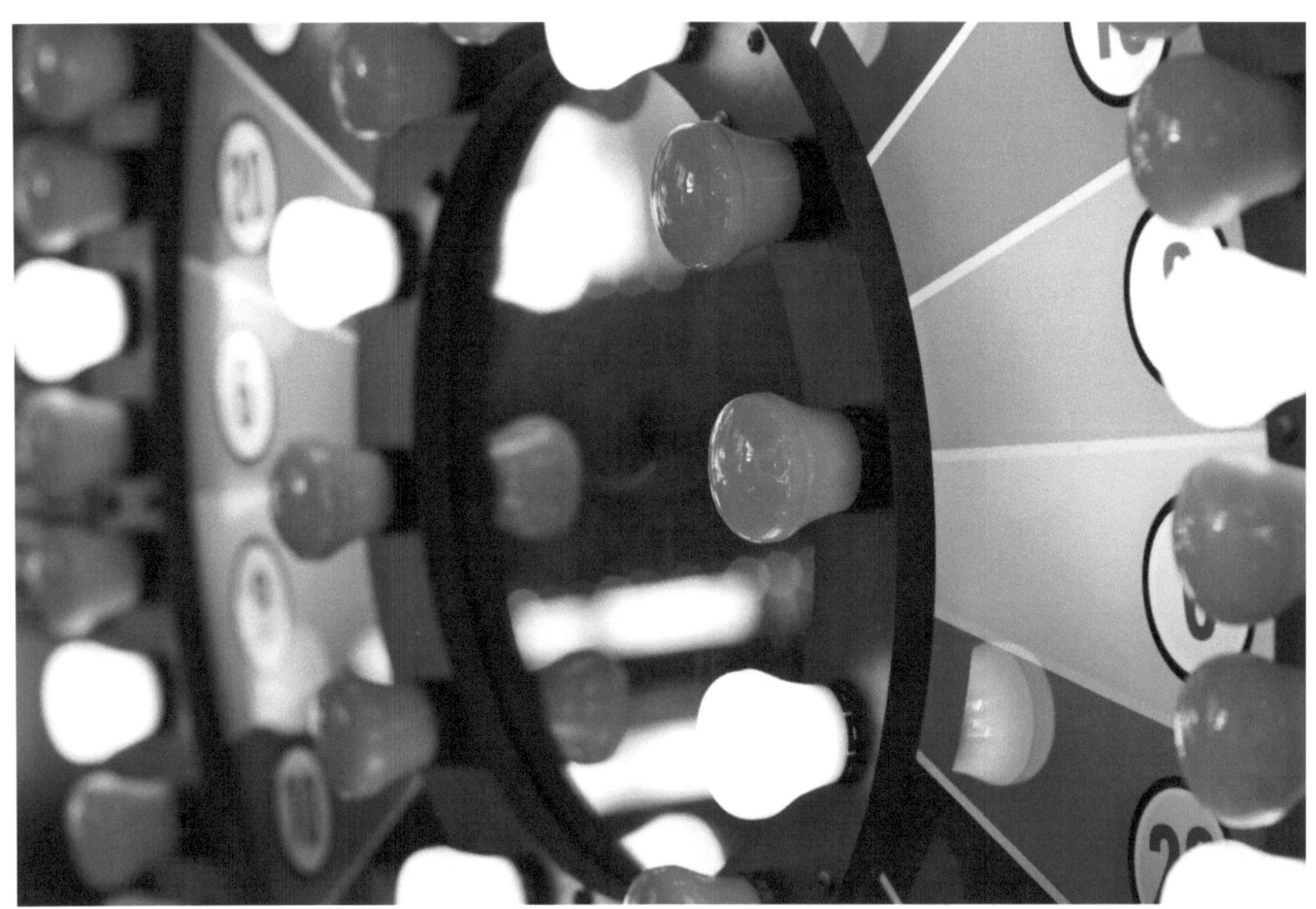

9980

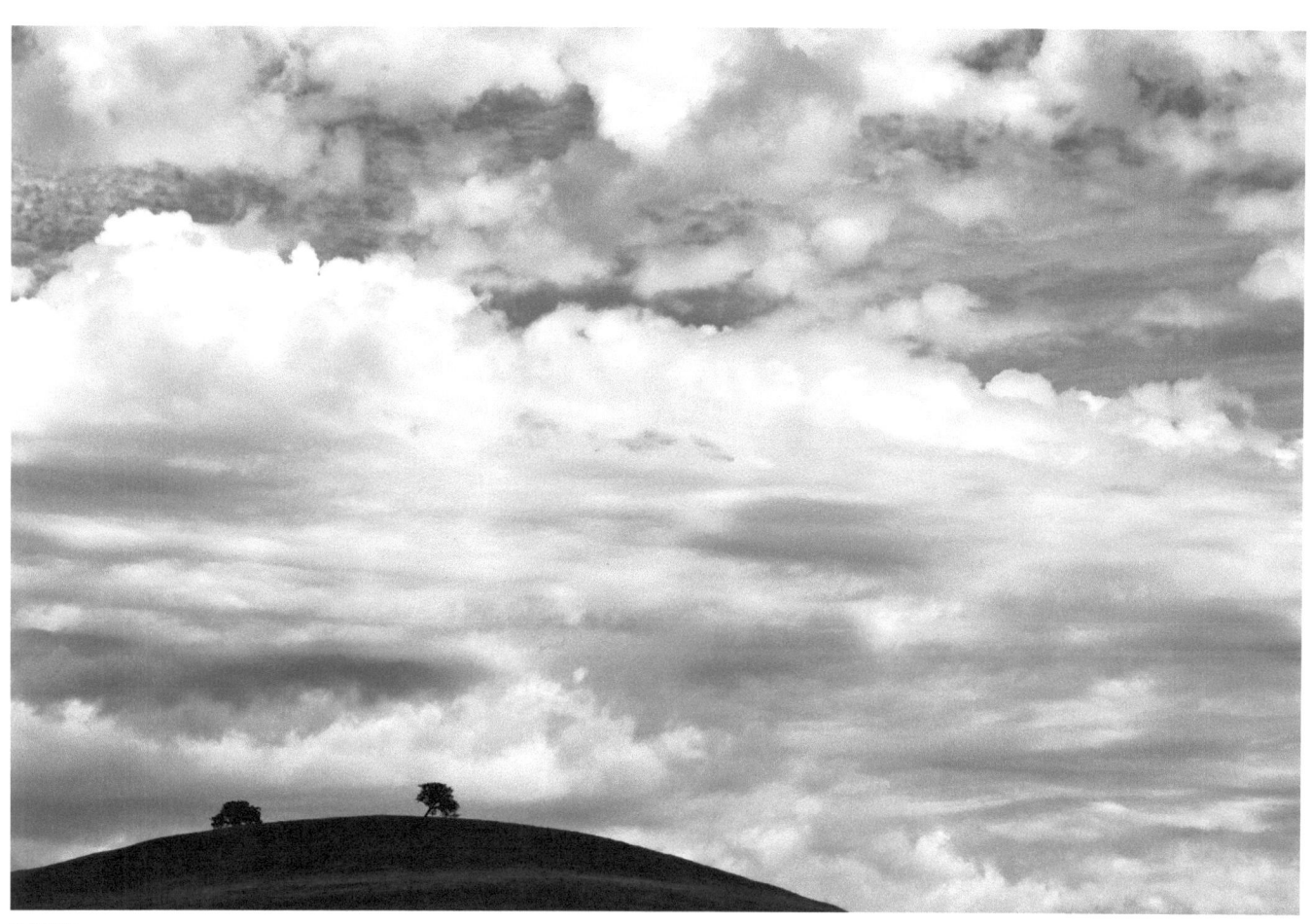

9992

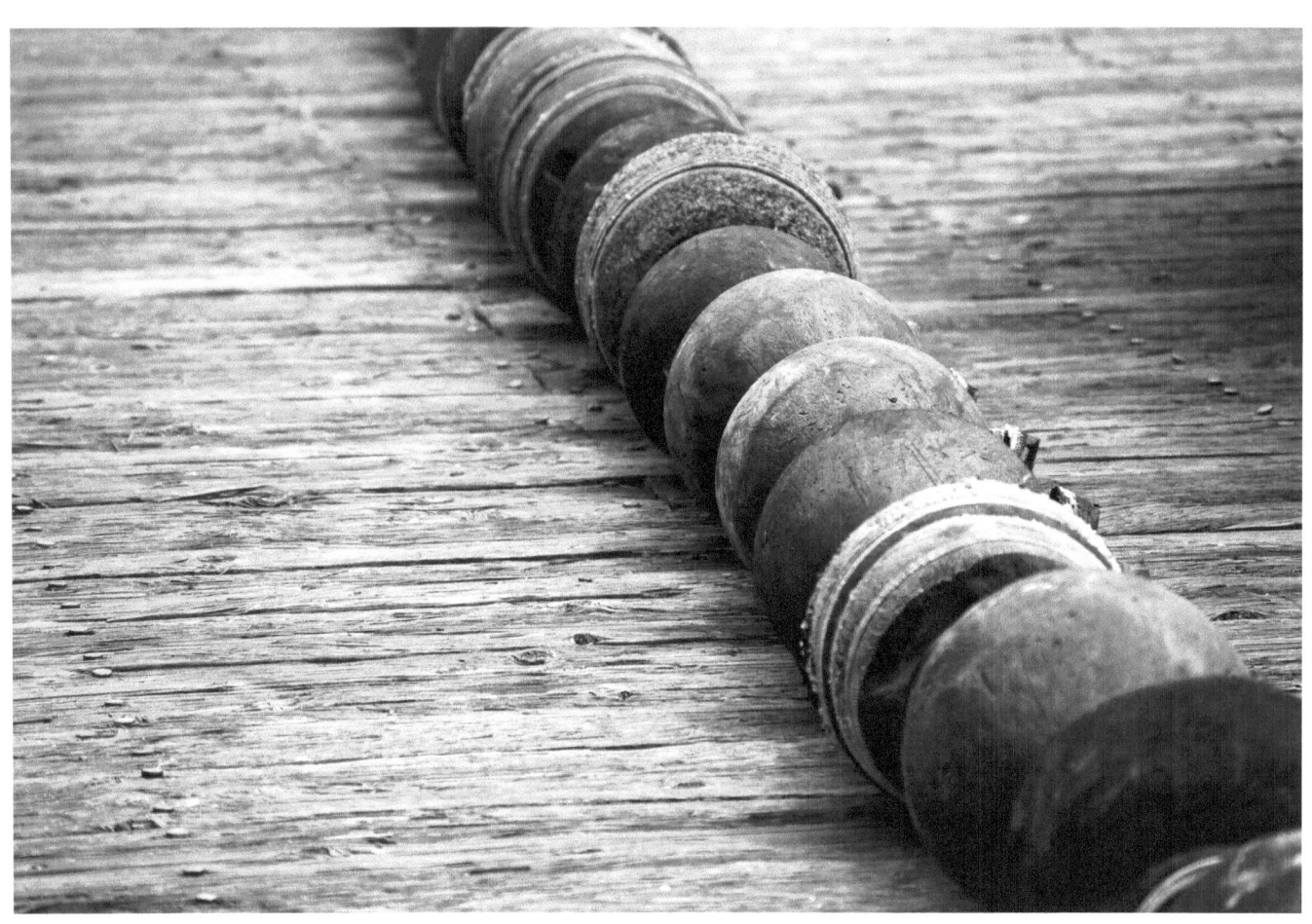

9998

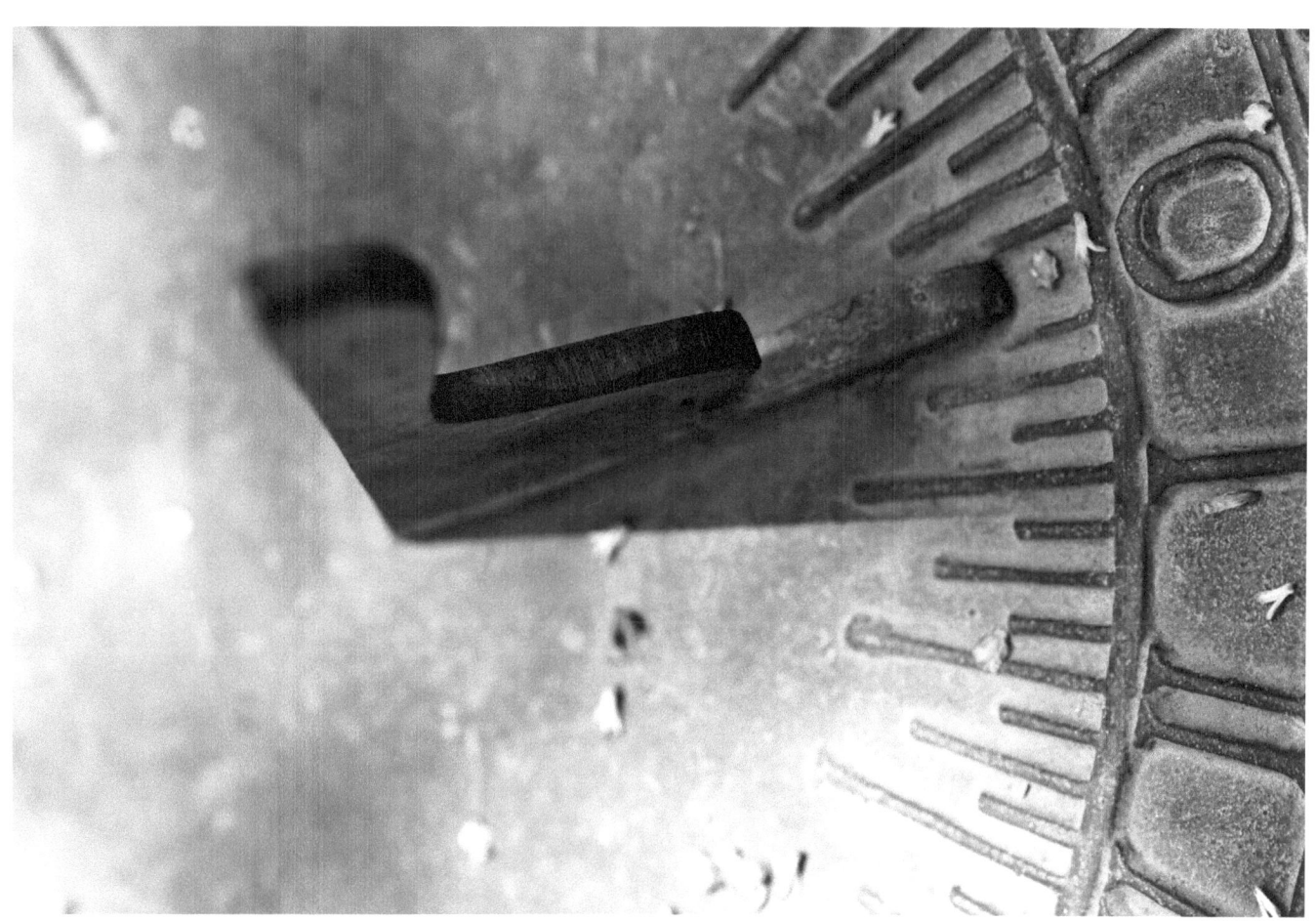

10002

www.ingramcontent.com/pod-product-compliance
Lightning Source LLC
Chambersburg PA
CBHW050802180526
45159CB00004B/1524